50 SIMPLE THINGS YOU CAN DO TO FIGHT THE RIGHT

EARTH•WORKS ACTION NETWORK

EarthWorks Press

This book is dedicated to Steve and Claire,
who have passed on their deep
commitment to progressive ideals.

Cover designed by Michael Brunsfeld.
brunsfeldo@comcast.net

ISBN: 0-9776897-0-0
First Edition 10 9 8 7 6 5 4 3 2

We've provided a great deal of information about
practices and products in our book. In most cases,
we've relied on advice, recommendations, and research
by others whose judgements we consider accurate and
free from bias. However, we can't and don't guarantee
the results. This book offers you a start.
The responsibility for using it
ultimately rests with you.

For more information, contact:
EarthWorks Press
P.O. Box 1089
Ashland, OR 97520
www.50simplethings.com

50 Simple Things® is a registered trademark
of EarthWorks Press

CONTENTS

FIRST AMENDMENT TO THE U.S. CONSTITUTION

"Congress shall make no law respecting an establishment
of religion, or prohibiting the free exercise thereof; or
abridging the freedom of speech, or of the press, or the right
of the people peaceably to assemble, and to petition
the Government for a redress of grievances."

FOURTH AMENDMENT TO THE U.S. CONSTITUTION

"The right of the people to be secure in their persons, houses,
papers, and effects, against unreasonable searches and seizures,
shall not be violated, and no Warrants shall issue, but upon
probable cause, supported by Oath or affirmation, and
particularly describing the place to be searched, and
the persons or things to be seized."

INTRODUCTION

For the past few decades the Right has generated most of the passion and energy in American politics. Progressives have sat passively by, watching as right-wing radicals have stood, jumped, yelled, and cursed us out.

We've become the new Silent Majority.

The result is that the public institutions which make up the core of our democracy—media, schools, churches, local government—have lurched to the Right.

If we want a healthy, balanced society, we have to pull these institutions back to where they belong...now. And the only way to do that is to generate the same passion and energy on the Left that they've been creating on the Far Right—to offset their influence on the culture with our own.

That's where this book comes in. As you'll see, it isn't written to convince people who disagree with us—we're not trying to change anyone's mind. It's an instruction manual for progressives; it offers specific things to do, to help you get active and stay active.

It doesn't matter which—or how many—Simple Things you pick. What matters is that you do *something*. Fifty-nine million Americans voted Democratic in the 2004 presidential election; if even a small percentage of them get active now, they can generate enough energy to change the direction of our country.

We've already done the first simple thing—collecting the information you'll find in this book, and putting it down as clearly and accessibly as we can. We've divided it into three sections: "Simple Steps" (the easiest things to do), "It Takes an Effort" (intermediate), and "For the Committed" (most difficult). Now the job is, literally, in your hands.

Times are tough, but we feel optimistic. We have an abiding faith in American democracy, and in the power of progressive ideals. We have no doubt that when you decide to act, the world will change. And if you haven't acted yet, it's probably because you didn't know *what* to do. We hope we've done our part to rectify that.

Now let's get going.

NOTES ON THE INTERNET

• The ideas included here came from people all over America. In February 2005, we sent out an e-mail asking friends to forward our request for "Fight the Right" suggestions to their friends...and to keep it going. We got hundreds of thoughtful, enthusiastic e-mails back. As a thank-you, at the end of the book we've acknowledged any contributors (or would-be contributors) who supplied their names. The rest of you know who you are...but we don't.

• You'll see right away that this book is chock full of URLs (Web site addresses). So if you don't have Internet service, or easy access to it, our apologies. But we assume most of you do...and when you start exploring, you'll find an amazing network of progressive activists on it. It's one of the things that kept us going during the year we worked on the book. When we felt tired or overwhelmed, we went online to read *Dailykos.com*, or *Talkingpointsmemo.com*, or Kevin Drum's *washingtonmonthly.com*, or a host of other political Web sites, and felt energized again. We believe you'll find the authentic voice of American progressives on the Web...and it will inspire you.

• Admittedly, some of the URLs are ridiculously long. We've tried to avoid this whenever possible—but detailed Web addresses are often the only way we can make sure we're sending you directly to a specific place on a Web site. Some of the best information on the Web is hidden; you can't find it unless you know exactly where you're going. However, if you just can't stand the endless URLs, you can always try using Google—enter the subject, the group, and any details we've supplied, and there's a good chance you'll find it.

• Unfortunately, there was no way to fit everyone into these 192 pages. We apologize to anyone who feels they should have been included. But we have good news on that front: our Web site—*www.50simplethings.com*—will enable us to add to the material...and this book will become just the tip of the everyday activist's iceberg. So let us know what you've got to share, and we'll get it into people's hands...or at least, onto their screens.

Hmm...Since we've got a space at the bottom of the page, we'll repeat that Web site address: *www.50simplethings.com.*

ABOUT THE DEMOCRATS

You'll note, as you read, that we seem to be steering people toward the Democratic Party rather than any third party. You're right. We were going to explain it; then we found this passage at the beginning of *Crashing the Gates*, by Jerome Armstrong and Markos Moulitsas Zúniga. They speak for us as well:

> Part of the present American reality is that we live in a two-party system, and the Democratic party is our only alternative. It's efficient—and expedient—to reform the existing party of the left, much as the conservative movement took over the Republican party in the 1970s and converted it into the electoral powerhouse it is today.

PROGRESSIVE VS. LIBERAL

You'll also notice that we refer to ourselves primarily as progressives, and only occasionally as liberals. The term "liberal" has taken quite a beating over the last decade or two, and it's going to take some work to rehabilitate it. We'll do it. But in the meantime, "progressive" is a great word…and an important part of our political heritage. The Progressive Movement of the late 1800s and early 1900s was America's first organized response to unchecked corporate power. It embodied the first political efforts to protect our natural resources. It actively tried to better the lives of America's working men and women—and their children—at a time when government showed little concern for them. Progressives invented the modern laws and regulations that protect consumers from unscrupulous business practices as well.

In the 1930s, FDR adapted the term "liberal" to describe his political programs, and we've been using it ever since. But the battle with the Right taking place today precedes the New Deal. We're back to fighting for worker's rights, for basic consumer protections, for a government that takes responsibility for the well-being of all its citizens and resources. To do that effectively, we need to resurrect the commitment and passion of the original Progressive Movement.

Sure, we're FDR and JFK liberals. But we're proud to call ourselves progressives…and this time we'll defend that term—and everything it stands for—as if it's a sacred trust. Because, as far as we're concerned, it is.

BASIC

TRAINING

WHY FIGHT?

"One thing is sure. We have to do something." —**FDR**

Most progressives agree that the Right is a serious threat to American democracy, and that we need to do something to stop them.

But while that may be obvious to you, some people are still uncomfortable with the idea of "fighting." They think it's too negative and too divisive.

So perhaps the first thing to do is explain why we think it's important for progressives to join forces and fight the Right. Here are three reasons:

1. We need to stand up for what we believe in.

Progressive values are under attack...and if we don't fight for them, who will? In this case, "fighting" means *committed action*, not necessarily conflict—a willingness to sacrifice and a determination to overcome obstacles.

Of course, "fight the Right" does imply we're fighting *against* something rather than *for* it. But under the circumstances, it's hard to separate the two. Like it or not, if we want to achieve our vision of a progressive America, we have to take on the Radical Right.

The Right is open about the fact that they'd like to make liberals and liberal ideas a thing of the past. "I tell people, don't kill all the liberals," Rush Limbaugh once said to his audience. "Leave enough around so we can have two on every campus—living fossils—so we will never forget what these people stood for."

That's the kind of thinking we're up against.

"One lesson about democracy stands out above all others," comments one thoughtful progressive. "Bullies...cannot be appeased. They have to be opposed with a stubbornness that matches their own." And that's why, at least for now, standing up for what we believe in means fighting the Right.

"Sometimes you've got to start a fight to win one." —Senator Paul Wellstone

2. **If we don't stand up and fight for what we believe in, no one will join us.**

Over the last few years, liberal politicians have compromised and backpedaled so much that many Americans aren't sure what we stand for. So it makes sense that fewer people identify themselves as liberals or progressives today—even when they agree with us.

We have to win them back…but we can't do it with words. We have to *show* our neighbors who we are by demonstrating passion, commitment, and clarity of purpose. Americans respond to a fighting spirit; no one wants to be on a team of wimps.

3. **Fighting is a part of the progressive tradition.**

Historically, *we're* the Americans who've fought for what's good and moral. Plenty of programs that people now take for granted were achieved only because progressives were willing to fight for them— usually against the Right. For example:

• *Child labor laws:* In 1900, more than two million American kids worked in horrible conditions, often for 12 hours a day. In 1904, Progressives formed the National Child Labor Committee. They demonstrated, lobbied, and litigated, and after 34 years they finally succeeded. In 1938, the first Child Labor Laws were passed.

• *The Minimum wage:* In 1933, progressives passed the first federal minimum wage law. When the Supreme Court struck it down in 1935, labor unions organized campaigns and fought to get it back.

• *Social Security:* By 1910, progressives were already fighting for "social insurance." It took the Great Depression and FDR to convince Americans that it was a viable idea; today it's regarded as the country's most successful social program ever.

• *Civil Rights:* Just 50 years ago, African Americans in the South faced brutal legalized discrimination. Liberal and progressive Americans of all races risked injury, jail time, and even death to eliminate this evil. In 1964, over the objections of many conservatives, the Civil Rights Act was passed.

We could go on, but you get the idea: progressives rise to the challenge when America needs help. And America surely needs help today.

"Faith is not belief. Belief is passive. Faith is active." —Edith Hamilton

WHO ARE WE FIGHTING?

We should make it clear that this book isn't an attack on conservatism. Any student of history knows that democracy needs both liberals and conservatives to maintain a healthy political balance. They're opposite sides of the same coin.

American conservatism, like American liberalism, isn't a dogmatic philosophy; it's a way of thinking—an approach to politics and life in general. Conservatives value the status quo and tradition; they're cautious about change and have a healthy skepticism of big government, but are committed to fair play and democracy.

Part of Our History

This country has always had warring liberal and conservative factions. In the 1780s, Hamiltonians (conservatives) and Jeffersonians (liberals) clashed bitterly about almost every aspect of government. But their commitment to American democracy transcended political ideology. And together, they managed to create the U.S. Constitution. This document was designed to enable both sides to flourish, to prevent either side from acquiring too much power, and to assure an active role for the political minority—whichever group it happened to be.

Clearly, the adage "the eagle needs a left wing and a right wing to fly" is historically and philosophically accurate. America has always embraced it wholeheartedly.

So if we're not fighting conservatives, who are we fighting?

THE RADICAL RIGHT

Today, America is increasingly dominated by groups that call themselves conservative...but aren't.

These groups don't even bother to pretend they're interested in caution or prudent changes anymore. "We are no longer working to preserve the status quo," announced Paul Weyrich, founder of the Heritage Foundation. "We are radicals, working to overturn the present power structure of the country."

These right-wing radicals have no respect for democratic traditions like bipartisanship.

"Bipartisanship is another name for date rape."
—Grover Norquist, *Americans for Tax Reform*

They have no interest in developing policies through debate and compromise:

"The Democrats—far too many of them—are evil, pure and simple. They have no redeeming social value. They are outright traitors themselves or apologists for treasonous behavior. They are enemies of the American people and the American way of life."
—Joseph Farah, *founder of the right-wing news service, WorldNetDaily*

And though they may mouth the rhetoric of conservatism, they have no allegiance to its principles. Small government? The U.S. government has grown by more than 33% since the year 2000. Fiscal responsibility? Our $230 billion surplus has been turned into a $412 billion deficit—an additional debt load that's almost three times the size of Russia's entire gross national product.

Eyes on the Prize

There's plenty more to say about them—and we will. But the most important point is this: The Radical Right's primary goal is gaining enough power to dismantle American democracy as we know it, and reconstruct it in their own image.

When a man like Randall Terry, founder of Operation Rescue, openly declares, "Our goal is a Christian nation. We have a biblical duty, we are called by God to conquer this country," you can believe he means it.

Extremists like these have always been with us. But today they're more dangerous than ever...because for the first time, they control most of the American government.

People who love America and love our democracy have only one option: Fight to stop them.

"If you're not a born-again Christian, you're a failure as a human being." —Jerry Falwell

RADICAL THOUGHTS

Think we're exaggerating when we describe the threat of the Radical Right? We're not...and the best way to prove it is to let them speak for themselves. Here's what prominent right-wingers think about...

AN INDEPENDENT JUDICIARY
• "Judges need to be intimidated. If they don't behave, we're going to go after them in a big way."
—Tom DeLay, *ex-House Majority Leader*

• "I'm a radical; I'm a real extremist. I don't want to impeach judges, I want to impale them."
—Mark Schwartz, *Republican activist and official spokesman for Sen. Tom Coburn (R-OK)*

SEPARATION OF CHURCH AND STATE
• "They (the 'Radical Left') have kept us in submission because they have talked about separation of church and state.... It's a lie of the Left, and we're not going to take it anymore."
—Rev. Pat Robertson, *The Christian Coalition*

ENVIRONMENTAL PROTECTION
• "I'd like to get every environmentalist, put 'em up against a wall, and shoot 'em."
—Bob Grant, WABC *talk-show host*

• "Environmentalism is a form of pagan fundamentalism. These green wackos are fanatics like al-Qaeda.... Osama believes there are 72 virgins waiting for him. The environmentalist believes human beings cause global warming. They both want to wreak havoc because of their mad beliefs. What's the difference?"
—G. Gordon Liddy, *radio talk-show host, convicted felon*

BI-PARTISANSHIP
• "You cannot cripple an opponent by outwitting him in a political debate. You can only do it by following Lenin's injunction: 'In

"When I see a tree, I see paper to blow your nose." —Rep. Don Young (R-Alaska)

political conflicts, the goal is not to refute your opponent's argument, but to wipe him from the face of the earth.'"

—David Horowitz, *Center for the Study of Popular Culture*

SANE FOREIGN POLICY

• "I'm almost going to come out in favor of war every 10 years, so that we always have a group of people in this country that know what it's like. It's not healthy to go without a war for all these many years, because you get people that are born and grow up, and don't know what one is, and then the war happens, you start firing ammunition, and they think the world is coming to an end. When the truth is we're kicking ass over there."

—Rush Limbaugh, *radio talk-show host*

FREEDOM OF SPEECH

• "Americans need to watch what they say, what they do."

—Ari Fleischer, *ex-White House press secretary*

PLURALISM

• "We are engaged in a social, political, and cultural war. There's a lot of talk in America about pluralism. But the bottom line is, somebody's values will prevail. And the winner gets the right to teach our children what to believe."

—Gary Bauer, *the Family Research Council*

• "What this is coming down to is who runs the country. It's us against them. It's the good guys versus the bad guys. It's the God-fearing people against the pagans."

—Randall Terry, *founder of Operation Rescue*

SOCIAL SECURITY

• "Hey, hey, ho, ho, Social Security has to go!"

—Republican activists, *chanting at a town hall meeting hosted by Sen. Rick Santorum (R-PA)*

Good news: 75% of young voters plan to be "more active in the political process in the future."

FOUR GROUND RULES

These rules are essential tools for anyone who wants to take on the Right or strengthen the progressive movement. Make them a part of any Simple Things you do. They'll help you avoid the pitfalls that have tripped up progressives in the past…and turn you into a more effective activist.

GROUND RULE #1: VALUES COME FIRST
Don't Forget What You're Fighting For

The focus of this book is issues and action. But keep in mind that *values* are at the core of the fight against the Radical Right. To fight effectively, you have to know what you believe in—what matters to you on the deepest level. For example:

- Do you believe in equal opportunity?
- Do you believe everyone deserves health care?
- Do you believe in the right to privacy?
- Do you believe in protecting the environment?

If you answered yes, then you've got progressive values. And *they* are what you're fighting for.

Progressives are deeply moral people, motivated by a profound sense of right and wrong. Don't lose sight of that. And don't let the right wing's chest-beating about *their* morality distract you. It's only spin.

Just be clear about what *you* believe. Remember as you go through this book that your moral sense is what's driving you. Your values are your strength.

You won't necessarily agree with other progressives about every issue, but you *will* find that you share a moral vision—that's what makes you progressives in the first place. Focus on your common morality rather than on your differences. Let it be a bond that unites you.

Remember: Your Values Are Traditional American Values
Never mind the right-wing propaganda; progressive values uphold

In 2004, the 7 Democratic senators who voted against the Iraq War were all reelected.

the best American traditions. We believe in freedom of speech, freedom of religion, civil rights, strong public education, separation of church and state, conservation, and transparency in government. The Radical Right talks a good game when it comes to values, but look what they've actually given us: secretive government, unilateral war, cronyism, fiscal irresponsibility, a polarized society. Which of these do you think Americans are most proud of? Which set of values makes America great? Don't forget that.

Once you're clear about your values, it's easier to articulate ideas and policies more forcefully. That leads to…

GROUND RULE #2: STICK TO YOUR MESSAGE

Take Control of the Debate

Ever notice how easy it's been for the Radical Right to provoke us? We get distracted by their rants, and pretty soon we're reacting to everything they say. That's not a great strategy; once an opponent has you reacting, you've lost the battle—because now you're not talking about your ideas, you're talking about *theirs*.

The trick is to stay focused on your own message. For example, if you say, "Bush has weakened all environmental regulations to benefit industry,"…and your opponent comes back with "All environmentalists are wackos," don't take the bait. Instead, focus on what's important to you. Respond: "Do you believe that our children should have clean air and water?"

Or suppose you're talking about the controversy around teaching "Intelligent Design," and your opponent pipes up with "All those teachers are just atheists." Instead of getting defensive, just steer the discussion back to where *you* want it to be. Ask: "Do you think it's important for the U.S. to keep its lead in science and technology?"

You get the idea. This applies to every issue. Stay on message and control the conversation. Present your own ideas, express your own values, and you'll inevitably offer a strong alternative to the messages of the Radical Right.

U.S. census statistic: Poverty in America has risen every year since Bush's tax cuts took effect.

When you've got words and ideas under control, you're ready for…

GROUND RULE #3: THINK STRATEGICALLY

Remember: You're Building a Movement

At the same time you're fighting the Right, you can be building the progressive movement. All you have to do is add a little strategic thinking to the mix.

Strategic thinking is knowing what your long-term goals are, and then figuring out what you can do to achieve them. It's the thread that ties your individual actions to something bigger.

What makes strategic thinking so effective is that it gives people in thousands of different communities a chance to informally join forces. All they need is a few shared goals and a commitment to fulfilling them. In the long run, the cumulative weight of a series of small, strategic actions can create an unstoppable political force.

Let's say, for instance, that our strategic goal is to elect a Democratic majority to Congress. You can volunteer for a campaign, of course—that's important. But it takes a lot more than good campaign volunteers to elect a candidate.

So what else do Democratic candidates need in order to be successful?

Here's one idea: To reach voters, our candidates need friendly media outlets. The Left doesn't have a propaganda machine like FOX News yet…but we do have Air America, a fledgling progressive radio network. If enough of us listen and support it, we'll make it a commercial success. Then we can count on Air America to be there during the next election, promoting Democrats and giving them a platform from which they can speak directly to the American people.

Moreover, once progressive talk radio is commercially viable, other progressive media outlets will emerge—giving our candidates even more coverage and a better chance to get elected.

So as you can see, one way you can fight the Right—and help elect Democrats—is to listen to the radio. Sounds easy? The power of thinking strategically is what turns a "Simple Thing You Can

Al Franken's political action committee: Midwest Values PAC (www.midwestvaluespac.org)

Do" into an effective political act.

Strategic thinking doesn't just strengthen the progressive movement; it also strengthens us as individual activists. Something special happens when we understand our actions in a larger context. It gives us a sense of purpose, which helps us persevere when things get difficult or frustrating. It inspires other people to join in. And it creates a sense of community, a feeling of connection to others who are doing the same thing.

GROUND RULE #4: THINK LONG-TERM
Remember: Don't Overdo It

There are so many worthwhile groups and activities asking for your help that it's easy to get overwhelmed. What should you do? Whom should you support? The only effective solution is to know your own limits and stick to them. Is there room in your budget to support only one group? Pick one and ignore appeals from the rest. You've got only a few hours a month to volunteer? Find one activity you like and focus on that.

Don't let yourself get burned out—a consistent effort over the long haul is what changes things. That should be your focus.

So, now that you're thinking long-term, what are your goals?

*   *   *   *

JUST REMEMBER...

"...You don't actually have to fight. Just courageously be who you are, with no apologies. You can put your progressive views out there without feeling obligated to debate or convert anybody. Just put 'em out there!"
—*Marc Cochran, Idaho*

Aesop said it 8,000 years ago: "United we stand, divided we fall."

STRATEGIC GOALS

Let's take a moment to consider what, in real terms, we hope to achieve. The EarthWorks Action Network has built this book around five strategic goals that are not only critically important to the progressive movement, but are also simple and reasonable. Think of them as tools to help you focus your energy and efforts on the most effective ways to protect America from the Radical Right.

1. RESTORE THE PROGRESSIVE VOICE IN AMERICA

The Radical Right complains about "liberal bias" in the media, but it's a phony issue. The truth is, the political "center" has moved so far to the right that people who would have been considered moderate 25 years ago are called ultra-liberal today.

Still, the attacks have been effective. Some liberals have been pummeled into silence. Others try to speak out, only to find less and less room for their voices in the mainstream media. By 2003, MSNBC-TV was so skittish about liberals that network execs chewed out one of their talk show hosts for having *two liberal guests in one week.*

Meanwhile, the Right's voice has gotten stronger. Over the last 30 years, they've built an alternative infrastructure to deliver, influence, and even create news that reflects their views. They have their own TV network (FOX News), virtual control of AM radio, well-funded print media, and "foundations" and "institutes" that churn out and publicize right-wing policies and positions.

The result: Our views—views shared by most people in the country—are rarely heard. It's time to level the playing field.

Solution: We need to find ways to tell America who we are and what we believe. This means building *and supporting* our own information-delivery infrastructure: Subscribing to progressive magazines, listening to progressive radio, supporting progressive blogs, watching progressive documentaries. We need to speak out more as individuals, too—talk to each other, share ideas, expand our community, and provide mutual support.

2. TAKE BACK PATRIOTISM

Attacks on our patriotism are part of a right-wing political strategy to undermine the credibility of our ideas by demonizing us. Progressives have tended to minimize the importance of this— we know we're patriots and we don't feel the need to prove it to anyone. But we've been fooling ourselves. For 25 years the Right has repeated their mantra: Liberals aren't real Americans; liberals are out of step with America; liberals are the "hate-America crowd." And eventually the branding of liberals as anti-American has become a serious obstacle to our regaining power. Even the term liberal—once a source of pride—has been turned into an epithet.

Solution: We need to make our love of America and American democracy a central part of our message and our public identity. Not only is this a declaration of who we are, it's a way to take direct aim at the Radical Right's strength. They've wrapped themselves so tightly in the American flag that they're convinced they're the only true patriots... and this bizarre self-identification has become one of the main building blocks of their ideology. Take it away from them, and they'll be seriously weakened.

3. PRESERVE HEALTHY COMMUNITIES

A healthy community is a place where people of all political views can come together to work for a common good, where public services like libraries and schools are supported, where there are plenty of public spaces for neighbors to meet and get to know each other. A healthy community promotes democracy, civic responsibility, and pluralism.

In short, it's the American ideal.

What does this have to do with fighting the Right? Well, most Americans support these things...but the Radical Right doesn't. They want to substitute their narrow view of American culture for the traditional inclusive, secular culture that has made our country flourish.

That's why a strong, cohesive community is a firewall against the spread of the Right.

Solution: We need to make our communities stronger by:
- Increasing participation in local democracy
- Supporting our public schools
- Joining civic associations and neighborhood groups
- Volunteering for community projects
- Strengthening liberal religious institutions to offset the Religious Right's influence

4. BUILD A UNITED MOVEMENT

One of progressives' greatest strengths is our "big tent"—we make room for a variety of political views. Unfortunately, it's also one of our weaknesses. We often wind up pulling in so many different directions that our power is diffused. We can even wind up fighting each other rather than our opponent.

Meanwhile, that opponent, the Radical Right, has been busy creating a strategic alliance that enables its deeply divided base— true conservatives, libertarians, neocons, and religious fundamentalists—to focus on common goals and put their differences aside. That, more than anything else, has been the source of their political strength.

FDR once said, "People acting in a group can accomplish things which no individual acting alone can even hope to bring about." The Right has demonstrated what can be accomplished when you join forces for a greater cause. They've also shown how easy it is to defeat us when we're divided.

Solution: We need to move past single-issue politics and create an alliance to fight the Right and promote progressive values. That means concentrating on the things we agree on, developing a mechanism for compromise and above all, delivering a message that Americans will recognize and embrace.

5. RESTORE A BALANCE OF POWER

In 1977, Democrats controlled the presidency and both houses of Congress. Today, Republicans have it all—and the Radical Right owns a big share of it.

How did they do it? "Many organizations worked together to gain control," says Gloria Totten of Progressive Majority. "They made a concerted, intentional, and strategic political effort. They didn't just focus on one strategy, one race, one body of power."

In 1978, for example, right-wing Republican funders created the GOP Political Action Committee (GOPAC) to recruit and train candidates for future elections; at the same time, religious groups like the Moral Majority and the Family Research Council began massive voter registration campaigns that helped strengthen the Republican Party.

In 1991, Rev. Pat Robertson told followers, "We are training people to be elected to school boards, to city councils, to state legislatures, and to key positions in political parties.... By the end of this decade, if we work and give and organize and train, the Christian Coalition will be the most powerful political organization in America."

It's unsettling to realize that the Right has been planning this takeover for so long. On the other hand, it's encouraging to know that even in politics, dedication and hard work pay off.

Solution: We need to build a political infrastructure to put Progressives in office—and keep them there. That means recruiting electable candidates, working on campaigns, and getting out the vote. It also means encouraging activists to step into positions of power in the Democratic Party—not just sit on the sidelines and complain. At the same time, we need to actively protect the democratic process; voting irregularities orchestrated by the Right are a threat to American democracy.

※　　※　　※　　※

HOPEFUL THOUGHT

"As my very Republican friends wrote on the card they enclosed with a small bouquet of flowers on November 3, 2004...'There is more that unites us than divides us.'"

—*Kathy Loehmer*

...and leave them in books and magazines in doctors' offices.

AND REMEMBER...

If your workplace is safe; if your children go to school rather than being forced into labor; if you are paid a living wage, including overtime; if you enjoy a 40-hour week and you are allowed to join a union to protect your rights—you can thank liberals.

"If your food is not poisoned and your water is drinkable—you can thank liberals.

"If your parents are eligible for Medicare and Social Security, so they can grow old in dignity without bankrupting your family—you can thank liberals.

"If our rivers are getting cleaner and our air isn't black with pollution; if our wilderness is protected and our countryside is still green—you can thank liberals.

"If people of all races can share the same public facilities; if everyone has the right to vote; if couples fall in love and marry regardless of race; if we have finally begun to transcend a segregated society—you can thank liberals.

"Progressive innovations like those and so many others were achieved by long, difficult struggles against entrenched power. What defined conservatism, and conservatives, was their opposition to every one of those advances. The country we know and love today was built by those victories for liberalism—with the support of the American people."

—Joe Conason, *Big Lies*

*   *   *   *

"It is up to us. So let's get off our butts and start
building a progressive movement. "
—Molly Ivins

SIMPLE

STEPS

1. IT'S YOUR CALL

Every year since 1986, Working Assets has donated 1% of its sales to progressive nonprofits. Total contributions to date: $50 million.

BACKGROUND. This is the first Simple Thing in the book because it's *really* simple: If you have long-distance service, or you're looking for a new wireless service, call an 800 number or go online and change your service to Working Assets.

What will that do? Well, you'll be supporting a company dedicated to progressive causes…contributing 1% of your long-distance or cell-phone bill to liberal groups…helping to establish progressives as an economic force…and sending a message to the business community that it pays to align themselves with progressives.

Not bad for a few minutes of effort.

AN ASSET TO THE COMMUNITY
• Working Assets began in 1985. Today, they're the model of a successful progressive company, with 300,000 long-distance customers.
• Working Assets has built their business around progressive politics. For example: With every bill, they send out action alerts highlighting two important political issues, and offer their customers free phone calls to elected representatives.
• **Result:** They've become a political force as well as a business. In 2005, their customers "generated nearly four million calls, letters and e-mails to Congress, the White House, and corporate leaders."

SIMPLE THINGS YOU CAN DO
• **Sign up for Working Assets long distance:** Call 1-800-227-0298 or go online to *www.workingassets.com* and click on "Long Distance," then on Join Now. For wireless, call 1-800-496-2942 or visit *www.workingassetswireless.com*. Rates are competitive.
• **Stay current:** Working Assets' online journal of progressive news and commentary is updated daily. (*www.workingforchange.com*)
• **Speak up:** Their activist Web site explores current issues and provides links to elected officials and businesses so you can make immediate comments. (*www.actforchange.com*)

Hold the phone: Verizon gives two-thirds of its political contributions to Republicans.

2. STRENGTH IN NUMBERS

"I'm declarin' war on the ACLU. I think they're a terrorist group.... Can I get some lawyers to help me out here? Can we sue 'em?" —Bill "The Bloviator" O'Reilly

BACKGROUND. There are plenty of ways we can build a united political movement. But none of them is easier—and few are more effective—than simply joining a progressive group. It's so easy, in fact, that you might wonder if it's worth doing.

The answer is an emphatic yes. Whether they're large (Planned Parenthood) or small (Friends of the Greensprings), these groups *need us*. Our support is what gives them the clout, credibility, and resources to make a difference.

We need *them*, too. When a bad law needs to be stopped... when our civil liberties are threatened...when right-wing propaganda needs to be countered, these are the people we rely on to step up and fight. They're the backbone of the progressive movement.

IN THE TRENCHES

Here's what progressive groups are doing for us...

• **Defending the Constitution:** If it weren't for the American Civil Liberties Union (ACLU) or the Center for Constitutional Rights, who'd stand with dissenters exercising their right to free speech? The ACLU handles 6,000 civil liberties lawsuits a year. Bonus: O'Reilly thinks they're as bad as al-Qaeda.

• **Protecting women's reproductive rights:** For decades, groups like Planned Parenthood and NARAL Pro-Choice America have protected *Roe v. Wade* from right-wing attacks. And no one is fighting harder for the morning-after pill. When, for political reasons, Bush's FDA refused to approve it, NARAL created their "Women Are Waiting" campaign to fight the decision.

• **Preserving the wilderness:** When the Bush administration tried to allow oil drilling in the Arctic National Wildlife Refuge, groups like the Sierra Club, NRDC, and MoveOn.org rallied members to

Financial power: MoveOn.org was the first group ever to raise $ix figure$ via the Internet.

send hundreds of thousands of e-mails and letters to Congress in protest. The drilling was stopped...and then it was stopped *again*.

• **Exposing the Right:** Groups like People for the American Way Foundation monitor Religious Right leaders and organizations to expose their extremism. When Pat Robertson declared that Israeli Prime Minister Ariel Sharon's stroke was God's punishment, for example, it was PFAWF that brought it to the world's attention.

• **Defending democracy:** If not for the NAACP, we wouldn't have "one person, one vote." And if you think that's an outdated issue, guess again. Today, the NAACP is leading the fight to help voters who were disenfranchised in the 2000 and 2004 presidential elections regain their voting power.

SIMPLE THINGS YOU CAN DO

The only hard part about this Simple Thing is deciding which group(s) to support.

Join National Groups: We've listed quite a few in this book. There are hundreds more we could recommend, and new organizations are forming every day. For a comprehensive list:

• *www.progressivemajority.org/news/links.asp*
• *www.publiceye.org/lnk_dem.html*
• *www.commondreams.org/community.htm*

Join Local Groups: They're not always easy to find, but it's worth looking for them. They do important work...and since they're always underfunded and understaffed, your contributions make a big difference.

• Many national organizations have Internet links to local chapters (e.g., Sierra Club *www.sierraclub.org*, ACORN *www.acorn.org*, Democracy for America *www.democracyforamerica.com*)

• Check out bulletin boards: physical (co-ops, bookstores, cafes, college campuses) and cyber (Yahoo Groups *www.groups.yahoo .com*, *Craigslist.org*, *Meetup.com*)

• Contact bloggers in your state (see page 74) for suggestions.

• Google your state or city name, plus "progressive group" or a specific subject (e.g., "environment").

"He whose ranks are united in purpose will be victorious." —Sun Tzu

UNDER ATTACK

Need a reminder of why it's important to support progressive groups? Read what these right-wingers have to say.

For the past few decades, the ACLU has been on a major crusade to destroy Christianity in America, promote filth under 'freedom of speech and expression,' and of course, vigorously defend the homosexual culture of death.... Perhaps it's time to recognize the ACLU as the American Communist Lawyers Union instead of their disingenuous 'civil rights' stage name."

— *Devvy Kidd,* WorldNetDaily

"The largest and most influential hate group in America, misnamed 'People for the American Way'...[wages] a permanent campaign of fear and hate aimed principally at Christian conservatives but at every group that attempts to defend America against the assaults of the Left."

— *David Horowitz,* FrontPage

"Planned Parenthood is not a benevolent organization trying to strengthen women's rights. It is a cold, calculating group intent on spreading the Humanist religion, luring our children into their Web of premarital sex and unlimited abortions, reducing the population of minorities in particular and filling its coffers with the profits from sales of birth-control devices."

— *www.jesus_is_savior.com*

"MoveOn.org is just another lunatic left Web site that has crossed the line and now provides aid and comfort to the enemies of the United States. MoveOn.org is probably the best friend that al-Qaeda has.... MoveOn.org is definitely anti-American."

— *Anonymous blogger, on Alexa.com*

"The NAACP should have riot rehearsal. They should get a liquor store and practice robberies."

— *Rush Limbaugh*

3. TAKE BACK THE LANGUAGE

"'When I use a word,' Humpty Dumpty said in a rather scornful tone, 'it means just what I choose it to mean—neither more nor less.'" —Lewis Carroll, Through the Looking Glass

BACKGROUND. One of the Radical Right's most effective strategies has been taking control of America's political vocabulary. They've redefined every word from "extremist" to "secular." And their crowning achievement is undermining our own political identity. "Liberal," which once signified a thoughtful, humane approach to policy, has entered the contemporary lexicon as "unpatriotic wimp."

Well, we've let them get away with it for 25 years, but enough is enough; it's time to take our words back.

LANGUAGE ARTS

• What's the big deal about controlling the language? "You don't just lose the words," says linguist George Lakoff, "you lose your ideas, because you no longer have a way to speak about them."

• The Right has understood this for a long time. In the mid-1990s, for example, Newt Gingrich sent two lists of words to Republican leaders. One was positive terms to use in describing Republicans (e.g., "courage," "family," "freedom"); the other was negative words to use on Democrats ("pathetic," "sick," "traitors"). It helped them take control of Congress a few years later.

• More recently, a Republican "playbook," created by GOP messaging guru Frank Luntz, was intercepted and posted on the Internet. In it, Luntz talks about "words that work" and how to use them to control the political dialogue. For example, he tells Republicans they should never say "drilling for oil"; instead, they should say "exploring for energy." By redefining phrases like these, the Right limits the debate in ways that are favorable to them…and takes away some of our most powerful rhetorical weapons.

Luntz's Republican messaging: "Never say 'Capitalism.' Always say 'Free market economy.'"

SIMPLE THINGS YOU CAN DO

Taking back the language isn't a science—it's an art; you have to experiment to see what works. A few ground rules:

• **Define your own words.** Some words are essential to any political dialogue: "freedom," "justice," "patriotism," "national security," etc. Decide what they mean to you, then defend your definitions. Protect your identity, too: Define "progressive" and "liberal" then insist on *your* meaning.

• **Understand what they're doing...**and make a conscious effort to fight it. Read Luntz's playbook online (Google "Luntz Playbook") and George Lakoff's *Don't Think of an Elephant.* Learn to recognize Luntz-type "messaging statements" when you hear them (e.g., "marriage penalty"). Pay attention to the nuances attached to words like "public," "private," "secular," and "values." Listen for Orwellian language. (See page 32.)

• **Challenge the use of right-wing messaging in the mainstream.** Make people conscious of what they're saying. If a newspaper uses a phrase like "death tax," write and complain. If your friends use it in conversation, point it out; ask if that's what they mean to say.

Three ways to take words back:

• **Replace them with your own definition.** Someone says: "The ACLU is an extremist organization." You redefine it in personal terms ("To me, an extremist is someone who blows themselves up; is that what you mean?") or directly ("The ACLU is a pro-American organization that defends the Constitution"). Keep using your own definition; ignore theirs.

• **Challenge them.** Most liberal-bashers parrot slogans without giving much thought to their meaning. If you make them explain every word, their rants fall apart. "Extremist? How are they extremist?" "Exactly which liberals are you talking about? Give me some examples."

• **Turn the tables.** Take control of their words. Redefine them: "Conservatives? Bush and his supporters aren't conservatives; they're *spendthrifts.* The GOP is the *Spendthrift Party.*" "The federal deficit? It's a *stealth* tax that transfers the burden to our kids." "National security? *National vulnerability* is more like it. We're more dependent than ever on foreign oil."

More Republican messaging: "Never say 'Trial Lawyer.' Always say 'Personal Injury Lawyers.'"

WAR OF WORDS

"Politics," said famed military tactician Karl von Clausewitz, "is war by other means." And one of the primary weapons in politics is words. Here are three examples of typical verbal battles.

SNEAK ATTACK

In his book *Reason*, Robert Reich points out a common right-wing tactic: "The Right charges liberals who look for ways to improve the country with 'blaming America first.' It's an old debater's trick: Impugn the motives of someone who levels a criticism, and shift the conversation away from the content of the criticism to the person making it." One way to respond: Talk about *their* motives. Restate the real issue, for example, and ask if they're just calling you names because they're afraid to talk about it.

ORWELLIAN ARMOR

In George Orwell's *1984*, Big Brother's totalitarian government controls its people in part by subverting the language. They use slogans like "War Is Peace," and "Freedom Is Slavery." Today, when the meaning of a word or phrase is turned upside down, we call it *Orwellian*. The Bush administration frequently uses Orwellian phrases: The "Healthy Forests" bill was actually a law that would make clear-cutting public lands easier; and the "Clear Skies" initiative made it easier for corporations to pollute the air. Keep an eye out for this kind of language. Why? When the Right uses an Orwellian approach, it's a sign they're afraid to reveal the truth. As George Lakoff explains, they're showing you "where they are vulnerable."

VERBAL AMBUSH

Watch out! Don't assume you and your opponent are talking about the same thing, just because you're using the same words. For example: You probably think that if you're a loving parent, devoted to your family, you have "family values." But you'll be caught off guard, because when it comes to defining "family values," how you relate to your family is irrelevant to the Radical Right—"family values" is actually code for opposition to abortion and gay rights. Best strategy: Think of each conversation as a verbal tug-of-war: If you're clear about the meaning of your words and can hold your ground by constantly restating your message, then you won't get pulled into their frame of reference.

Word alert: If someone on the Right calls it "the *Democrat* Party," it's an attack—correct them.

MAJORITY REPORT

It's part of the Radical Right's strategy to label their opponents "extremists," and repeat the epithet so often that it becomes part of the cultural lexicon. But it's just wishful thinking on their part. If you've come to think of yourself as being out of the mainstream, it's time to think again: You're part of the American majority in many important ways, and it's the Far Right that's out there on the fringe.

62% of Americans say they would prefer a universal health care system to the current program. (*ABC News poll*)

69% of Americans favor "providing more generous government assistance to the poor." (*Pew Research*)

66% of Americans don't want *Roe v. Wade* overturned. (*Wall Street Journal*)

83% of Americans support raising the minimum wage. (*Gallup*)

84% of Americans support right-to-die laws. (*Pew Research*)

58% of Americans consider "dealing with the nation's energy problem" a top priority…and 82% favor increased federal funding for research on wind, solar, and hydrogen energy. (*Pew Research*)

68% of Americans consider "reforming the public schools" the way to handle education. Only 23% favor "finding an alternative." (*Gallup*)

77% of Americans say that "the country should do whatever it takes to protect the environment." Only 18% disagree. (*Pew Research*)

65% of Americans feel "the right to privacy has either been lost or is under serious threat." (*Public Agenda*)

67% of Americans say Bush does not have a clear plan for handling the situation in Iraq. (*CNN/USA Today/Gallup*)

76% of Americans approve of Social Security. (*Harris*)

85% of Americans support our National Park System. (*Harris*)

Poll results: 64% of Americans pick the Statue of Liberty as our greatest symbol of patriotism.

4. SUPPORT THE WATCHDOGS

Bill O'Reilly: *"Can you give me one example where I smeared someone?"*
John Podesta: *"How about referring to Al Franken as Joseph Goebbels?"*

BACKGROUND. Right-wing political hacks like Rush Limbaugh used to be able to tell any lies they wanted to on the air, and no one would hold them accountable.

But things have changed. Today there are watchdog groups that listen to everything people like Limbaugh say, and then post the lies, half-truths, and omissions on the Web. Bill O'Reilly, for example, can tell a whopper on Wednesday night, and by Thursday it will be posted, word for word, on Media Matters. O'Reilly rails furiously at these "left-wing smear sites" but doesn't challenges them on their facts…because he can't.

Progressive watchdogs are not only effective at controlling the Right's news spin…they're also great entertainment. And they're an important piece of the emerging progressive media. As long as we support them, they'll keep watching.

FUN WITH BILL O'REILLY
Let's use Bill to demonstrate two of our favorite watchdog tricks:
1) Sniffing out lies: Bill has endorsed a boycott of France…
O'Reilly (to a Canadian reporter): "Now if…your government harbors these two [U.S.] deserters…there will be a boycott of your country, which will hurt your country enormously. France is now feeling that sting…. [T]hey've lost billions of dollars in France according to *The Paris Business Review.*"
Media Matters comments: *"[We] found no evidence of a publication named* The Paris Business Review…. *Furthermore, contrary to O'Reilly's claim that France has lost 'billions of dollars' due to an American boycott, American imports from France have actually increased since international tensions with France began."*

2) Retrieving outrageous comments: Our media watchdogs are on hand to dig up comments that O'Reilly tries to bury. Like these:

• "If al-Qaeda comes in here and blows [San Francisco] up, we're not going to do anything about it. We're going to say, look, every other place in America is off limits to you, except San Francisco. You want to blow up the Coit Tower? Go ahead."

• "All those clowns over at the liberal radio network, we could incarcerate them immediately. Will you have that done, please? Send over the FBI and just put them in chains, because they, you know, they're undermining everything."

• "I just wish Katrina had only hit the United Nations Building, nothing else, just had flooded them out, and I wouldn't have rescued them."

SIMPLE THINGS YOU CAN DO

Read the watchdog sites: It's a revelation to see just how far the Right's talkers have been "stretching the truth."

Spread the word: Be creative and e-mail your favorite right-wing lies as a periodic "Top 10" list or as "O'Lie-lly Alerts" (Note: Always tell people where you got the info, so they can check it out themselves).

Support them financially: All of these Web sites are at least partly supported by donations. Contributions help keep them going.

Respond: Let people know you're paying attention. Media Matters and other sites provide contact info at the end of each article, so you can e-mail the shows they quote or the groups involved.

Be a watchdog: Is there a media person in your area who spreads right-wing misinformation? Take action; to find out how, check out Media Matters' online Action Center and see page 139.

RESOURCES

• **Media Matters for America** (*www.mediamatters.org*)
• **News Hounds—"We watch FOX so you don't have to."** (*www.newshounds.us*)
• **FAIR** (*www.fair.org*)
• **The Daily Howler** (*www.dailyhowler.com*)
• **Crooks and Liars** (*www.crooksandliars.com*)

"I don't consider myself an offensive guy. I'm just a harmless, lovable little fuzzball." —Rush Limbaugh

5. A PUBLIC OFFERING

*In 2003, Mother Jones was a National Magazine
Award finalist for General Excellence…and The Nation
won the award for Best Columns and Commentary.*

BACKGROUND. Want to spread a political message and support progressive media at the same time? Instead of taking something *out* of your local library, put something *into* it—pool resources with some friends and give your local library a subscription to a liberal magazine.

DID YOU KNOW?

• The $10–$30 you spend on a subscription (depending on the publication) is a great investment: Library subscriptions build credibility for small progressive magazines, make their news and commentary available to thousands of new readers, and increase their circulation substantially.

• For example: *Washington Monthly*, an influential political journal, has a paid circulation of only 23,600. If 1,000 people contribute subscriptions, circulation will increase by almost 5%. That's an enormous benefit to them.

• Z, another small progressive magazine, offers this advice: "If you want to buy a subscription for your local library, try to find a library that doesn't already carry [the magazine], so you can expose new readers to it. Before buying the subscription, you should check with the reference librarian [to be sure] that they will display the magazine if you sign them up. The librarian will probably want to see a copy of the magazine, if they are not already familiar with it, before agreeing to carry it—even if you are buying the subscription for them. So be prepared to show them an issue."

Insider tip: Since magazines aren't usually checked out of the library, librarians tend to evaluate the popularity of a periodical by how often they have to reshelve it. So next time you're in the library, do a little guerrilla marketing—flip through a progressive magazine, then leave it on a table.

RESOURCES

Here are 10 progressive magazines that every library should have. They all need your support: Circulation figures refer to print only; many also have a large online readership. For example: The online version of In These Times *gets 350,000 hits a month.*

• **Mother Jones.** Cost: $10 for 7 issues. Circulation: 250,000. The biggest of the outspoken progressive mags. Subscriptions: *www.motherjones.com*

• **The Progressive.** Cost: $19.97 for 12 issues. Circulation: 60,000+. Began as an opposition voice to McCarthyism in the 1950s. Subscriptions: *www.progressive.org* or 1-800-827-0555

• **Washington Monthly.** Cost: $29.95 a year. Circulation: 23,600. Insider political commentary. Subscriptions: *www.washingtonmonthly .com* or 1-877-POLITIX (1-877-765-4849)

• **Z Magazine.** Cost: $33 for 11 issues; $18 online. Circulation: 17,000. Subscriptions: *zmagsite.zmag.org/helpz.htm*

• **In These Times.** Cost: $24.95 for 12 issues. Circulation: 17,000. Subscriptions: *www.inthesetimes.com* or 1-800-827-0270.

• **E/The Environmental Magazine.** Cost: $19.95 for 6 issues. Circulation: 50,000. Subscriptions: *www.emagazine.com*

• **The Nation.** Cost: $29.97 a year, 47 issues. Circulation: 187,000. Subscriptions: *www.thenation.com* or 1-800-333-8536

• **Extra!** Cost: $21 for 6 issues, plus 6 issues of *Extra!Update*, FAIR's bimonthly magazine of media criticism. Subscriptions: *www.fair.org/index.php?page=106* or 1-800-847-3993

• **The American Prospect.** Cost: $19.95 for 12 issues and a free e-subscription. Circulation: 55,000. *www.prospect.org* (click on "subscribe") or 1-888-687-8732

• **Utne Magazine.** Cost: $12 for 6 issues. Circulation: 225,000. Subscriptions: *www.utne.com/subscribe*

And be sure to check out: *www.newpages.com/altmags*—a complete listing of alternative publications.

Want to laugh? *Funny Times* (www.funnytimes.com) is a progressive humor review.

THE "CHICKEN-HAWK" BRIGADE

It's the worst kind of hypocrisy when you avidly encourage others to do what you refused to do. Big surprise: Many of today's most vocal conservative hawks did not serve.

PROMINENT REPUBLICANS

• **Speaker of the House Dennis Hastert:** Avoided draft, did not serve

• **Former House Majority Leader Tom DeLay (R-TX):** Avoided draft, did not serve

• **House Majority Whip Roy Blunt (R-MO):** Did not serve

• **Sen. Majority Leader Bill Frist (R-TN):** Did not serve

• **Senate Majority Whip Mitch McConnell (R-KY):** Did not serve

• **Rick Santorum (R-PA), third-ranking Republican in the Senate:** Did not serve

• **Former Senate Majority Leader Trent Lott (R-MS):** Avoided draft, did not serve

• **Former House Speaker Newt Gingrich (R-GA):** Avoided draft, did not serve

• **Jeb Bush, Governor (R-FL):** Did not serve

• **VP Dick Cheney:** Several deferments—the last by marriage (in his own words, "had other priorities than military service")

• **Karl Rove:** Avoided draft, did not serve

THE FIGHTING 101st TALKING HEADS

• **George Will:** Did not serve

• **Bill O'Reilly:** Did not serve

• **Paul Gigot:** Did not serve

• **Bill Bennett:** Did not serve

• **Pat Buchanan:** Did not serve

• **Michael Savage:** Did not serve

• **Bill Kristol:** Did not serve

• **Sean Hannity:** Did not serve

• **Rush Limbaugh:** Did not serve (4-F with a "pilonidal cyst")

6. SIGN THEM UP

In six states—Minnesota, New Hampshire, Idaho, Maine, Wisconsin, and Wyoming—eligible citizens can register to vote on Election Day.

BACKGROUND. Since you're reading this book, it's a safe bet that you're already registered to vote. But more than 30 million Americans over the age of 18 aren't—and according to some studies, a majority of them would vote for progressive candidates…if only they were registered.

So here's a simple challenge: Find one or two of these potential political allies before the next election and help them become voters.

IT'S EASY

You don't have to be anything "official" to register someone to vote. Anyone can do it. In most states, all you need are a national voter registration form…and a person to register.

To register this way, however, a person does need a driver's license or Social Security number. If they don't have either, contact your local County Clerk for more instructions.

Two ways to get a Voter Registration Form:

(1) Get one from the League of Women Voters or local election officials. You might also find them at public libraries, post offices, unemployment offices, public high schools, or universities.

(2) Get one online, from the Federal Election Commission (FEC). Go to *www.eac.gov/register_vote.asp* and download or print pages 2–5 of the registration form. Each state has its own voter registration rules and deadlines. Find yours on pages 8–32. *Note: It's a PDF file; numbers refer to Acrobat Reader pages.*

SIMPLE THINGS YOU CAN DO

Adopt a Voter

• Find a person who's not registered but really wants to vote. It could be a neighbor, coworker, family friend, a parent of one of your child's friends, or someone who just turned 18.

Trickle-up theory: Studies show that if an 18-year-old votes, his or her parents are also likely to.

• Try to find out why they haven't registered, so you can work with them. Some people, for example, assume registering will be too difficult. Some just can't find the time. Some don't feel "qualified" to vote—they don't know all the candidates and think they're required to vote for every person or measure on the ballot; others just don't believe their vote means anything.

• Don't just hand them a form and tell them to mail it in. Help them fill it out, then mail it for them (or turn it in online). The election office will notify them about their polling location.

• As the election nears, make a date to review the issues and candidates over coffee or on the phone. Get a sample ballot and demonstrate how to mark it.

• See it all the way through: Volunteer to go to the polls with them. (See page 68.)

Guerrilla Voter Registration

• Feeling ambitious? Mount your own registration drive and sign up 5, or even 50, new voters. Great step-by-step instructions from Slacktivist (*www.slacktivist.typepad.com/slacktivist/2003/11/guerrilla_voter*) and RegisterFiveDemocrats.com, a grassroots Web-based group (*www.registerfivedemocrats.com*)

• Or join an organized group registration effort. Call local Democrats or the groups listed below for more info.

RESOURCES

• **League of Women Voters Education Fund:** (*www.smartvoter.org*)

• **Your Vote Matters (Working Assets):** Easy Web site, organized by state. (*www.yourvotematters.org*)

• **The National Low-Income Housing Coalition:** They have a good summary (and links) for group registration. (*www.nlihc.org/vrem/registration*)

• **Voter registration training:**

    —**Project Vote** (*www.projectvote.org*)

    —**NAACP** (*www.naacpnvf.org*)

    —**America Votes** (*www.americavotes.org*)

"Bad officials are elected by good citizens who do not vote." —George Jean Nathan

"HERE'S WHAT *I* DO…"

Three testimonials from some of the hundreds of grassroots activists who sent us their ideas for this book.

I TAKE A BREAK from a cup of joe once a week and donate the $3 that I save to Planned Parenthood, to keep access to our reproductive rights. I know that's only $12 a month, but think of how it would add up if a million people did it."

—*Marina Saga,* California

"THE FIRST TIME I EVER WROTE a letter to the editor was in the 1970s, when I lived in Vermont. Patrick Leahy had just been elected senator. One day someone sent a letter to our local newspaper criticizing Sen. Leahy, and I got so upset that I spontaneously wrote a response, defending him. It was printed. About a week later, at 6:30 A.M., my phone rang. I groggily answered, and an operator said 'Please hold for Senator Leahy.' He came on the phone and thanked me for my letter. I was in shock…but of course it taught me that officials really do pay attention to letters to the editor. So my advice is, let people know what you think—you never know who's listening!"

—*Jay Byrd,* Oregon

"I WORK NEXT TO AN OLD SCHOOL that offers free English classes, GED programs, and adult high school. For six months before the election, I kept a sign on their front door and on my door about registering to vote. People could drop in any time and I'd help them register. Then I'd address the form myself and pay for the stamp. I figured each 37¢ I spent was a vote against Bush. My mother did the same thing once a week in a movie theater in a low income neighborhood, my sister-in-law helped register people by visiting the bus transfer point downtown during rush hour. The forms are available free online, complete with instructions and addresses for all the county offices. Registration never takes more than a minute and you get to have a conversation with someone interesting."

—*Joann McCracken,* Michigan

Idea for activists: Put your congressperson's local phone number on speed-dial. Call frequently.

7. MONEY TALKS

Costco and Wal-Mart are rivals in politics, too: In 2004, Wal-Mart gave 82% (over $1 million) of its political contributions to Republicans. Costco gave 95% to Democrats.

BACKGROUND. How do you usually decide what products to buy and where to buy them—quality?...convenience?...price?

If you want to strengthen the progressive voice in America, there's another factor to consider: politics. All too often, the money we spend winds up going to companies that contribute to the Radical Right. If you buy Exxon gas, for example, you're also making a donation to the anti-environmental groups they support.

Of course, you don't always have a choice. But when you do, why not take advantage of it? Nothing attracts attention in America like money. So let's use our dollars to make businesses listen to, and respect, the progressive point of view.

BE A "BLUE" CONSUMER

"Buying blue" means patronizing businesses that support progressive causes or candidates, and avoiding the ones that don't. Here are some criteria you might consider:

• **Political contributions:** Do they favor one party? You might be surprised. For example: In 2004, Hyatt Hotels gave 94% of its contributions to Democrats; rival Marriott gave 82% to Republicans.

• **Political causes:** What special interests do they fund? Did you know, for example, that the owners of Blue Diamond Almonds contribute heavily to Families for Conservative Values, a right-wing Florida group? Or that Progressive Insurance really is progressive?

• **Corporate policies:** Environment, labor, and corporate responsibility count. Did you know that Kroger, America's largest grocery chain, lets pharmacists refuse the "morning-after" pill to rape victims?

• **Media ads and sponsorships:** Who do they sponsor? Geico used to advertise on Rush Limbaugh's programs, but pulled their ads after protests.

SIMPLE THINGS YOU CAN DO

Research. There's no simple equation you can use—you have to gather information, then make choices based on your values.

The resources below will get you started. They offer a good overview of the issues and plenty of detailed information.

Help build the BuyBlue movement:

BuyBlue.org is the national group behind the effort. To help them become a potent political and economic force...

• *Become a BuyBlue member or donor.*

• *Contribute information.* BuyBlue depends on members to collect and share data. Your research helps others make good choices.

• *Start a BuyBlue Local chapter.* Their goal is to have a chapter in each state, gathering information about companies doing business locally. The first local chapter: BuyBlue Colorado. Contact them to learn more: *www.buybluecolorado.org*

Contact Businesses:

• This is what gives us power. Calling or faxing has maximum impact...but e-mail works, too. Tell them what you plan to do in response to their political position, and why. Stick to the facts. Tell them what kind of business you've brought them and who you'll patronize instead. BuyBlue offers contact information.

• Remember: You don't have to go cold turkey. If you disagree with a company's policies but don't want to stop buying their product, exercise your right as a consumer—pressure them to change.

• Send a copy of your communication to BuyBlue. They'll put it in their files and create a record for others' reference.

RESOURCES

• **BuyBlue:** Building a community of progressives who vote with our wallets. *www.buyblue.org*

• *Shop at Your Own Risk,* by David Bernstein. Good introductory article. Find it at: *www.bostonphoenix.com* (*Search for title*)

• **Sourcewatch** *www.sourcewatch.org*
• **Public Citizen** *www.citizen.org*
• **Public Integrity** *www.publicintegrity.org*

For Shopping:
• *www.Alonovo.Com*
• *www.globalexchange.org*

THE WAR ON FREE SPEECH

Little by little, it seems that our right to dissent is being abridged. If we don't stand up for free speech, who will?

DISSENT: According to *Editor and Publisher* magazine: "Laura Berg, a clinical nurse specialist [at a VA hospital] for 15 years, wrote a letter in September (2005) to a weekly Albuquerque newspaper criticizing how the Bush administration handled Hurricane Katrina and the Iraq War. She urged people to 'act forcefully' by bringing criminal charges against top administration officials, including the president."

GOVERNMENT RESPONSE: She was investigated for *sedition*. "The VA seized her office computer and launched an investigation," *Editor and Publisher* reported on Feb. 11, 2006. "Berg is not talking to the press, but reportedly fears losing her job." The ACLU commented: "Sedition? That's like something out of the history books." They added: "Is this government so jealous of its power, so fearful of dissent, that it needs to threaten people who openly oppose its policies with charges of 'sedition'?" Sen. Jeff Bingaman (D-NM) demanded an investigation.

DISSENT: In September 2005, DailyKos.com reported that "Selina Jarvis, chair of the social studies department at Currituck County High School in North Carolina, assigned her senior civics and economics class a project: Take photographs to illustrate their rights in the Bill of Rights.... One student cut a photo of George Bush out of a magazine and tacked the picture to a wall with a red thumb tack through his head. Then he made a thumb's down sign with his own hand next to the President's picture, and he had a photo taken of that, and pasted it on a poster.

"According to Jarvis, the student, who remains anonymous, was just doing his assignment, illustrating the right to dissent. The student took his film to a local Wal-Mart to be developed, and a Wal-Mart employee called the police. The police turned the matter over to the Secret Service."

"Those who are ready to sacrifice freedom for security ultimately will lose both." —Abraham Lincoln

GOVERNMENT RESPONSE: The Secret Service then came to Currituck High. First, they took the poster. Then they talked to Ms. Jarvis. "They asked me, didn't I think that it was suspicious," she recalls. "I said no, it was a Bill of Rights project."

"At the end of the meeting, they told her the incident 'would be interpreted by the U.S. Attorney, who would decide whether the student could be indicted,' she says. The student was not indicted, and the Secret Service did not pursue the case further."

DISSENT: On Jan. 31, 2006, the AP reported: "Cindy Sheehan, the mother of a fallen soldier in Iraq who reinvigorated the antiwar movement, was invited to attend president Bush's State of the Union speech by Rep. Lynn Woolsey (D-Calif.). She arrived wearing a T-shirt bearing the antiwar slogan '2,245 Dead—How Many More?', which referred to the number of U.S. troops killed in Iraq, and covered it up until she took her seat."

GOVERNMENT RESPONSE: Just before Bush gave his speech, she was arrested, handcuffed, and removed from the House gallery. The charge: "demonstrating in the Capitol building." The wife of Rep. C.W. Bill Young (R–FL) was also removed from the gallery because she was wearing a T-shirt that read, "Support the Troops—Defending Our Freedom." But she wasn't arrested.

"As it turns out, Sheehan's arrest was illegal. Police got the U.S. attorney's office to drop the charges. 'We screwed up,' a Capitol Police official said, speaking on condition of anonymity. He said Sheehan didn't violate any rules or laws."

DISSENT: In 2005, a spokesperson for the organization that represents 48 state air pollution control agencies testified to a U.S. Senate committee that the "Clear Skies" initiative—part of the Republican effort to overhaul the Clean Air Act—was "far too lenient" on polluters and would undermine "states' abilities to protect air quality."

GOVERNMENT RESPONSE: Committee Chairman Sen. James Imhofe (R-OK) immediately demanded to see the group's tax and financial records. However, his staff assured reporters that it had "nothing to do with" intimidation.

"In a democracy, dissent is an act of faith." —Sen. J. William Fulbright

8. POLITICAL THEATER

In 2004 and 2005, 16 progressive political documentaries were released nationally in movies theaters—the most ever.

BACKGROUND. *Outfoxed*, a documentary exposing the right-wing bias of FOX News's "fair and balanced" coverage, premiered on July 13, 2004.

But it wasn't screened in a single theater. Instead, the film debuted in 3,500 living rooms across America as part of a "House Party" campaign created by MoveOn.org. Within a few weeks it had hit the top spot on Amazon.com's DVD best-seller list...and permanently changed FOX News Channel's public image.

This project was an important step toward restoring the progressive voice in America. It established a grassroots, do-it-yourself distribution system that put hard-hitting, politically potent documentaries directly into people's hands and homes. Now you can help keep it going.

POLITICAL POWER
Documentaries are a key piece of the emerging progressive media:

• They reach audiences with information the corporate media won't touch, examining controversial issues like the run-up to the war in Iraq (*Weapons of Mass Deception*) and the Patriot Act (*Unconstitutional: The War on Our Civil Liberties*).

• They offer in-depth, investigative reporting. "Audiences crave the information to navigate through these times," says *Outfoxed* producer Robert Greenwald. "The primary media is not doing it, because they're doing 30-second sound-bites. I think they've underestimated the craving people have for substance."

• They're persuasive. In 1988, for example, *The Thin Blue Line* got Randall Adams, a falsely convicted murderer, off death row. In 1998, Michael Moore's *The Big One* showed young children making shoes for Nike in Indonesia; as a result, Nike instituted a minimum age of 18 in its Indonesian factories.

In 2004–2005, seven progressive films grossed over $2.5 million apiece in theaters—a record.

SIMPLE THINGS YOU CAN DO

You *are the distribution system for progressive films. A few ways to spread the word (and perhaps influence elections in the future):*

• **Donate a documentary:** Give a progressive DVD to your local public library, high school library, or college library...or all three.

• **Request progressive documentaries:** Local video stores get the message that progressive videos are good business when you ask for them, watch them, and encourage friends to rent them.

• **Join the Ironweed Film Club:** Each month they'll send you a new progressive documentary. Host a screening, then pass your DVD on to friends. Cost: $14.95/month, $159.90/year: *www.ironweedfilms.com*

• **Borrow a film and host a screening:** The Film Connection is a "National Public Film Library." They help you set up screenings, then loan you films for free: *www.thefilmconnection.org*

• **Get a Move On:** Host a house party when MoveOn.org promotes a new documentary, or just go to one in your community.

• **Write a letter:** Ask local newspapers (see p. 77) to print your recommendations for documentaries, especially at election time.

RESOURCES

These Web sites sell documentaries and/or offer advice on setting up screenings:

• *www.filmstoseebeforeyouvote .org* (an old, but good list)

• *www.mediarights.org/tour/ enthusiast*

These just sell documentaries:

• *www.buyindies.com*

• *www.indiedocs.com*

10 RECOMMENDED DOCUMENTARIES

More info? Visit Web sites under film names (e.g., *www.outfoxed.com*)

• *Outfoxed: Rupert Murdoch's War on Journalism*
• *Bush's Brain*
• *The Control Room*
• *Orwell Rolls in his Grave*
• *Wal-Mart: The High Price of Low Cost*

• *Uncovered: The Whole Truth About the Iraq War*
• *Unconstitutional: The War on Our Civil Liberties*
• *Weapons of Mass Deception*
• *The Corporation*
• *Fahrenheit 9/11*

Don't miss this new documentary...*The Big Buy: How Tom DeLay Stole Congress.*

PROTECTING RELIGIOUS FREEDOM

You've probably heard it often: The Religious Right believes America was founded as a "Christian nation." Here's basic info you need to answer that false assertion, from the Web site TheocracyWatch.org

THE CONSTITUTION VS. THE DECLARATION

In 1789, after spending more than three months debating and negotiating what should go into the document that would govern our land, the framers drafted a constitution that is, in the literal sense, secular. There's no ambiguity about this. The historical record is clear.

However, people sometimes get confused about the Founders' intent because they don't distinguish between the Constitution and the Declaration of Independence. It's important to understand the difference.

The Declaration of Independence is not the document that established the United States as a new nation. It was written by Thomas Jefferson in 1778, nine years before the U.S. Constitution. It was signed by the Continental Congress and sent to King George III of England. It's a very eloquent document that's celebrated every July 4th...but it is not the law of the land. It is a statement of sentiments directed to the King in reaction to unfair taxation.

BUT WHERE'S GOD?

Foes of the principle of separation of church and state often refer to the word "Creator" in the Declaration of Independence as proof that the framers of the U.S. Constitution intended for the United States to be ruled by a sovereign being. Nothing could be further from the truth. As Rob Boston of Americans United for Separation of Church and State writes:

> What the Religious Right doesn't tell people, and what, tragically, many Americans apparently don't know, is that when it comes to determining what the laws of the United States mean, the only document that matters is the Constitution. The Constitution, a completely

72% of Americans believe "a great deal" or "somewhat" that their family relationships...

secular document, contains no references to God, Jesus, or Christianity. It says absolutely nothing about the United States being officially Christian. The Religious Right's constant appeals to documents like the Declaration of Independence, which contains a deistic reference to "the Creator," cloud the issue and make some people believe their rights spring from these other documents.

Another way of putting it: The Constitution is the one and only Official Rule Book of the United States of America. Not the Declaration. Not the Mayflower Compact. Not the Northwest Ordinance. And certainly not the Bible. The people who attended the Constitutional Convention considered all of the events and information that preceded it, and came up with a single document that established the ground rules for our nation. To reiterate: They did not include God, the Bible, or Jesus as part of it.

SECOND-GUESSING THE FOUNDERS

Members of the Religious Right generally claim to revere the Founders. Yet they seem to think that these able men simply *forgot to mention* Christianity. Or, more to the point, that the Founders *didn't bother* mentioning Christianity or the Bible in the Constitution because it was *understood* that America is a Christian nation.

This affront to the men who created our country—the idea that they might neglect to be explicit about something as significant as the role of religion in one of the most important documents in the history of the world—isn't worth taking seriously.

One ironic note: Many on the Radical Right consider themselves "strict constructionists" in matters of the Constitution—which means that they believe in interpreting the Constitution literally, not reading meaning into it.... Except, apparently, in this instance.

Two Facts from *The Godless Constitution,* by I. Kramnick and R.L. Moore

• "The preamble of the Constitution invokes the people of the United States. It does not invoke any sort of God."

• "The Constitution forbids any religious test to hold office. A godless person is just as eligible as a godly one! (Article 6, Paragraph 3.)"

... have been strengthened by religion.

9. RECLAIM THE BIBLE

"The biggest thing the Religious Right doesn't want you to know about the Bible is that whenever someone—Pat, Jerry, or anyone else—tells you what the Bible means, they're just interpreting it."
—Dr. Douglas Ottati, Union Theological Seminary

BACKGROUND. Whatever you believe about the Bible, it's important to recognize that much of its text can be interpreted to support progressive ideals. Of course, you won't hear that on shows like *The 700 Club* and *Focus on the Family*.

The Christian Right has been waging a furious campaign for the last 30 years to convince America that the Bible is "their" document. The result is that much of the public thinks that people who are truly religious *have to be* right-wing. But nothing could be further from the truth...and it's time we let people know it.

THE PROGRESSIVE BIBLE
Here are some examples of the Bible's liberal side. These aren't aberrations—the Bible is full of them.

Social justice? "Woe to those who enact evil statutes, And to those who constantly record unjust decisions, So as to deprive the needy of justice, And rob the poor of My people of their rights, So that widows may be their spoil, And that they may plunder the orphans."
—Isaiah 10:1–3

Tax cuts for the rich? "He who oppresses the poor to increase his wealth and he who gives gifts to the rich—both come to poverty."
—Proverbs 22:16

Protecting the environment? "You should not defile the land which you inhabit."
—Numbers 34:35

Tolerance? "Do not judge, and you will not be judged; do not condemn, and you will not be condemned. Forgive, and you will be forgiven; give, and it will be given to you."
—Luke 6:37–8

"Every good Christian should line up and kick Jerry Falwell's ass." —Barry Goldwater

Foreign policy? "Let us therefore follow after the things which make for peace."

—**Romans 14:19**

"Integrity will give peace, justice and lasting security. My people will live in a peaceful country."

—**Isaiah 32:16**

SIMPLE THINGS YOU CAN DO

Read the Bible: "If you want to focus on a few sections," says Dr. Douglas Ottati, "read what Jesus says in the Sermon on the Mount (Matthew 5–7, and parallels in the Gospel of Luke). If you're interested in social justice, read the Book of Amos. When you're done, ask yourself what this book says about the basic values that underlie our present government policy."

Learn the Right's positions: Go to Christian Right sites and see what they say. "If you want to understand the Religious Right, read Revelations," says Rev. Brad Bunnin. "It's the source of much of their theology. Progressives, on the other hand, tend to focus on Jesus' words. There's quite a contrast."

• Learn how to use the Bible to refute the Right. Get familiar with parts of the Bible that support progressive values and morality. Start with "Would Jesus Love a Liberal?" (See below.)

• Dissect the Right's rhetoric. They sound so authoritative, you may be surprised at how convoluted their interpretations are. For example, check out Jerry Falwell's article "God is Pro-War" at *www.worldnetdaily.com/news/article.asp?ARTICLE_ID=36859*

And whenever someone on the Right declares the meaning of the Bible, ask: "According to whom?" That's a good place to start.

RESOURCES

• **Would Jesus Love a Liberal?** (*www.timeforachange.bluelemur.com/liberalchristians.htm*) A comprehensive site that looks at the Bible from a liberal perspective.

• **Metaverse** (*www.zompist.com/meetthepoor.html*). Quotes on social justice.

See page 86 for more resources.

10. STICK IT TO 'EM

According to a 2003 survey, about 1/3 of private American vehicles are adorned with at least one patriotic bumper sticker or decal.

BACKGROUND. Ever notice that when you see a car with a flag flying, or a "God Bless America" bumper sticker, you assume it's being driven by someone on the Right?

Why is that? After all, it's our flag, too.

The Right has been claiming the symbols of American patriotism as their exclusive property for too long; it's time to take them back. With just a car and two bumper stickers, you can jump-start the process.

A BUMPER CROP

• Bumper stickers are a surprisingly effective form of mass media. If only 1,000 people see your message each week, you'll still reach more than 50,000 people a year. One thousand stickers will be seen over five million times.

• Bumper stickers have an impact. An extreme example: In 2004, a Denver cop told a woman to remove a strident anti-Bush bumper sticker from her pickup. When she refused, the cop illegally threatened to arrest her. A reporter witnessed the exchange and the next day it was news. As a result, the Denver police department wound up creating a program to instruct officers on free speech.

• Bumper stickers reinforce your own sense of political identity—and at the same time, they let other progressives know they're not alone.

SIMPLE THINGS YOU CAN DO

• First, find a bumper sticker with a positive progressive message that you like: "Proud to be a Democrat," "Another Patriot for Public Education," "My Family Values: Clean Air and Water." Then choose a no-nonsense patriotic bumper sticker or decal: "God Bless America," "United We Stand," the American flag.

• Put them right next to each other on your bumper or in your

What tradition? The words "under God" didn't appear in the Pledge of Allegiance until 1954.

window. Every time someone sees your vehicle, they'll get the message that you *do not* cede patriotism to the Right. The more often they see this combination, the more they'll subliminally associate the flag with progressive values. It's a small step…but it's an effective one.

Some Alternatives
Don't want to put a sticker on your bumper? Try one of these:
- Tape the stickers to the inside of your rear window.
- Use decals or electrostatic stickers (see below).
- Use window paint (available at most hardware stores).

Note: If you're not sure you'll be able to get a sticker off once it's on your bumper, here's some useful info. According to the Do It Yourself Network, to remove a bumper sticker, you:

1. Heat the sticker with a blow dryer ("high" setting).

2. Push the sticker up with an old credit card. "Keep heating and pulling and it should come right up. The top layer…may come off first; if so, just do the same thing to the bottom layer."

3. For more information, check out *www.diynetwork.com*, *www.popularmechanics.com*, or *www.ehow.com* and search for "Remove Bumper Stickers."

RESOURCES
Order progressive bumper stickers online. If you can't find the perfect one in stock, you can order a custom sticker for $5–$10.

- *www.carryabigsticker.com*
- *www.northernsun.com*
- *www.irregulartimes.com*

Stock or Custom
- *www.makestickers.com*
- *www.timsbumperstickers.com*
- *unemployeddemocrats.com*
- *www.goodstorm.com*
- *www.evolvefish.com*
- *www.bumperart.com*

- Stock or custom removable vinyl stickers and decals: *www.kartattooz.com*

- Emblems (car plaques) available for $5–$7 each at *www.evolvefish.com*

- Try individual groups; for example, The Interfaith Alliance offers a free "One Nation. Many Faiths" sticker. (*www.interfaithalliance.org*)

Good political advice: "Have fun." —Cass Sunstein

THE WAR ON INFORMATION

*Thomas Jefferson said, "Information is the currency of democracy."
So what does that say about a right-wing culture that tries to keep
information from its citizens? In a democracy, we expect transparency
in government. Here's a sample of what we've been getting instead.*

An obsession with secrecy. "Since President Bush entered
office, there has been a more than 75% increase in the
amount of government information classified as secret
each year—from 9 million documents in 2001 to 16 million by
2004." —*www.FreePress.net*

Fake "Facts." "The most commonly used curricula in abstinence-
only sex-ed programs financed by the federal government promote
'false, misleading, or distorted information.' They teach, for example, that masturbation can lead to pregnancy, that a third of the
time condoms fail to prevent transmission of HIV, and that HIV
can be spread through sweat and tears." —**Esther Kaplan, *With
God on Their Side***

Gagged Scientists. In 2005, James Hansen, director of the prestigious Goddard Institute for Space Studies, asserted publicly that
global warming is real and that the U.S. needs to lead the world in
reducing CO_2 emissions. This contradicts the Bush administration's
official policies. Shortly after, NASA headquarters let him know
there would be "dire consequences" if he continued to speak out.
(He ignored them.)

Fake News. "At least 20 federal agencies have produced and distributed 'video news releases,' using a $254 million slush fund set up
to manufacture taxpayer-funded propaganda. These bogus...stories
have been broadcast on TV nationwide without any acknowledg-
ment that they're prepared by the government rather than local
journalists. The segments trumpeted administration 'successes,'

promoted its controversial line on issues like overhauling Medicare, and featured Americans 'thanking' Bush. And they've been repeatedly labeled 'covert propaganda' by investigators at the Government Accountability Office." —*www.FreePress.net*

No Information. "The Bush administration has stopped enforcing the Freedom of Information Act (FOIA), and made it harder for reporters to do their jobs by refusing to cooperate with even the most basic requests for comment and data from government agencies. This is part of a broader clampdown on access to information that has made it virtually impossible for journalists to cover vast areas of government activity."

How did the Dept of Justice react when the administration disregarded the law? "In 2001, Attorney General John Ashcroft issued a memorandum advising federal agencies that the Justice Dept would defend their decisions to deny FOIA requests."—*www.FreePress.net*

Rigged Press Conferences. "The White House Press Office turned press conferences into parodies by seating a friendly faux journalist, former male escort Jeff Gannon, amid reporters and then steering questions to him when tough issues arose. They refuse to answer tough questioners such as veteran journalist Helen Thomas, effectively silencing reporters who might challenge the president or his aides." —*www.FreePress.net*

A Gag Order on Weather Reports. Even weather reports? After the Katrina fiasco, the Bush administration came up with a new rule: Employees of the National Weather Service couldn't talk to reporters unless the Department of Commerce approved it. "Under this new policy, the department, rather than the weather agencies, would also determine who would then provide comment."

"It does appear the intent of this policy is to restrict the flow of weather information to the national media," said a puzzled weather service employee—anonymously, of course.

—*Raw Story (www.rawstory.com)*

And don't forget Dick Cheney's secret energy task force. Check out: *www.projectcensored.org/publications/2005/8.html*

The White House censored 28 pages of the Congressional 9/11 report.

11. CONSIDER THE ALTERNATIVES

"A number of recent studies show that 40% of newspaper content—or more—is the result of organized PR campaigns." —**John Stauber, SourceWatch**

BACKGROUND. Are you getting enough of what you'd honestly call "news" from your newspaper or TV? Sad to say, our mainstream news sources seem more focused on "info-tainment" than on information these days.

At the same time, the Right's propaganda machine is systematically undermining reputable news organizations. Not only has the Bush administration actually paid journalists to lie, even traditionally reliable newspapers like the *New York Times* have been compromised by "government sources." The *Times*'s reporting on Iraq's weapons of mass destruction, based on administration misinformation, was actually used by Vice President Cheney to legitimize our invasion.

Without aggressively independent news sources to monitor it, our government can operate in virtual secrecy. And that means it can get away with almost anything. Fortunately, there are still independent sources of news.

NEWS VIEWS

• The Bush administration has made an art of burying unfavorable news with the "Friday night news dump"—releasing it on Friday afternoon because "fewer people read papers or watch TV over the weekend." By Monday, it's often forgotten.

• Why do the media let them do that? Perhaps because most are owned by a few huge conglomerates. All of the largest U.S. TV networks, for example, are owned by just five companies: General Electric, Viacom, Disney, News Corp., and TimeWarner.

• This may also be why so many controversial news stories are ignored—or appear only in alternative media. Want proof? Check out Project Censored's annual report of the Top 25 Censored Stories of the Year. (*www.projectcensored.org*)

"Everyone is entitled to their own opinions, but not their own facts." —Sen. Pat Moynihan

CHECK OUT THE ALTERNATIVES

What's out there? These three sites list multiple resources:

• **World-newspapers.com** Great site. International newspapers (*www.world-newspapers.com/index.html*) plus 40 news alternatives (*www.world-newspapers.com/alternative-news.html*)

• **Z *Magazine* alternative press** (*www.zmag.org/welused.htm*)

• **Western Libraries Alternative/Mainstream News Sources** (*www.library.wwu.edu/ref/subjguides/peace/alternative.htm*)

Individual Progressive News Sites
The cream of the crop of the Net's progressive news and commentary:

• **Alternet** (*www.alternet.org*)

• **Raw Story** (*www.rawstory.com*)

• **Truth Out** (*www.truthout.org*)

• **Common Dreams** (*www.commondreams.org*)

• **Smirking Chimp** (*www.smirkingchimp.com*)

• **Buzzflash** (*www.buzzflash.com*)

• **TomPaine.com** (*www.tompaine.com*)

• **Guerrilla News** (*www.guerrillanews.com*)

• **Think Progress** (*www.thinkprogress.org*)

• **Salon** (*www.salon.com*)

• **News you may have missed** (*www.newsdesk.org*)

Five Media Critics

• **Media Channel** (*www.mediachannel.org*) Everything for the media addict—criticism, news, investigative reporting.

• **PR Watch** (*www.prwatch.org/cmd/prwatch.html*) Dedicated to investigative reporting on the propaganda-for-hire industry.

• **Cursor.Org** (*www.cursor.org*) Insightful, clear analysis of media accuracy and political slant.

• **Columbia Journalism Review** (*www.cjr.org*)

• **The Nieman Watchdog Journalism Project** (*www.niemanwatchdog.org*)

In his first five years in office, President George W. Bush was on vacation for 11 months.

12. HEAR, HEAR!

"I like to listen. I have learned a great deal from listening carefully. Most people never listen." —**Ernest Hemingway**

BACKGROUND. If you're fed up with our polarized society, it's not so hard to do something about it. You can't change the way people talk to each other in Washington, but you *can* change the way people talk to each other in your own neighborhood.

It all starts with listening.

Taking the time to let other people share their points of view isn't just a way to get along with your neighbors, it's also astute political strategy. Listening promotes respect, cooperation, and civil dialogue. These are fundamental elements of a healthy democracy…and a healthy democracy is the ultimate progressive goal.

HEAR, HEAR

Let's be honest—no matter how noble your intentions, it can be pretty hard to listen to people you disagree with. So it's a good idea to learn a few skills to make you a better listener. For example:

Get physical.

• *Eye contact shows you're actually paying attention.* It's good to make eye contact with the speaker, but it can be hard to maintain. Helpful hint: Instead of constantly looking a person right in the eyes, focus on their eyebrows. It's a lot easier.

• *Try to control your reactions.* Maintain a neutral facial expression and body posture. Relax your hands. Posture counts, too; people equate sitting up straight with paying attention.

• *Maintain an "open" body position.* Folding your arms can be a subtle statement that you're closed to the speaker's ideas.

Be encouraging.

• *Small acknowledgments keep people talking.* Respond occasionally (but don't interrupt) with comments like "Okay" or "Uh-huh." Nodding your head works, too.

Q: What do Barbara Bush, Bill Clinton and Sandra Day O'Connor have in common?

• *Ask open-ended questions (but not too many)*. Get the speaker to clarify what they're saying with simply worded questions, using their own language or terminology, such as, "What do you mean by _____?" Don't challenge or judge. Remember: The point is to understand *their* ideas, not defend your own.

• *Try paraphrasing*. If you can't follow their logic, paraphrase what you think they're saying and let them confirm or correct it. For example: "So you see vouchers as a way for parents to have more control of their children's education?"

SIMPLE THINGS YOU CAN DO
Practice listening.
Try using these techniques in day-to-day conversation. They're easier to master when you don't feel like arguing with everything a speaker's saying.

Get some insight.
• Some progressives believe that if they can just explain their ideas, people on the Radical Right will "come around." The Right probably thinks that way, too. But this is more than a disagreement about policies and issues—Left and Right often have different world views…which is why they propose wildly different solutions to the same problems.

• Take advantage of the opportunity to explore the underlying viewpoints that shape the Right's opinions. It will make you a better neighbor and a more effective political activist.

• Three excellent (and short) books may help: *Don't Think of an Elephant*, by George Lakoff; *Reason*, by Robert Reich; and *Stick Your Neck Out*, by John Graham.

Stay focused on the result you want.
• Remember: You're listening to create understanding and mutual respect—a secure platform on which you can build healthy community.

• Side benefits: You may find that you have more in common with your neighbor than you expected. Plus, understanding what they think (and why) can help you clarify your own beliefs. It forces you to think through the reasons why you agree or disagree.

A: They each won "Listener of the Year" awards from The International Listening Association.

13. ADOPT A CANDIDATE

Q: *In 2002, what was the average cost to mount a successful campaign against a congressional incumbent?*
a) *Money doesn't affect elections*   **b)** *$5,000*   **c)** *$1.6 million*

BACKGROUND. You might think that if you live in Arizona, you can't support a candidate running for Congress in Michigan...or a city council candidate in Washington state. But today it's not only possible—it's essential.

People like you have become the Democrats' secret weapon. Progressive candidates all over the country know there's a network of activists, linked together by the Internet, who'll help them challenge the Radical Right. In a sense, there are no local elections anymore—every congressional race has national implications; every state and municipal race has an impact on how America handles key issues, from redistricting to environmental protection.

You can't support every worthy candidate, of course, but you *can* pick a few in pivotal races and "adopt" them. A victory by progressives in Minnesota or New Hampshire is a victory for all progressives. Remember: We're a movement.

MAKING A DIFFERENCE

• The Internet reached a turning point as a political tool in May 2005. Paul Hackett, an Iraq vet, ran for Congress as a Democrat in Ohio's 2nd District. Republicans usually get 70% of the vote there.

• The national party wrote him off, but liberal blogs created an Internet fund-raising campaign for him. Responding to the appeals, some 6,630 people from all over the U.S. "adopted" Hackett. In a matter of days, they'd contributed over $450,000—enough cash to enable him to wage a viable campaign.

• It wasn't a Cinderella story—Hackett lost. But he nearly pulled off an unthinkable upset; the Republican scraped by with only 52% of the vote...and the "netroots" (Internet grassroots) had new muscle. "We're giving lie," wrote the Daily Kos blog, "to the notion that we ought to simply surrender certain districts because they are 'too Republican.'"

Quiz answer: C...of course.

SIMPLE THINGS YOU CAN DO

Do a little research: Familiarize yourself with the races for House and Senate around the country. And pay attention to tight races in your state legislature—they're critical. (See page 175.)

• The quickest and best places to gather accurate info are Web sites like the ones listed below. If you want to back potential winners, you need to read about various races and learn to differentiate between typical campaign rhetoric and real information.

Adopt a candidate (or two, or three): Find candidates you like, and support them as if they were running in your district. The most important thing you can do is donate money. Do some fund-raising, too—contact people on your e-mail list and let them know why you're supporting these candidates.

• Regardless of where in the U.S. the candidate is running, you can help the campaign by going to their Web site and volunteering to make last minute "get out the vote" calls.

RESOURCES

• **Act Blue:** (*www.actblue.com*) Great online fund-raising site; the only tool of its kind. Makes it possible for anyone to start an online fund-raising campaign like MoveOn's.

• **Progressive Majority:** (*www.progressivemajority.org*) Recruits and trains progressive candidates at the local level.

• **EMILY's List:** (*www.emilyslist.org*) Promotes pro-choice Democratic women candidates.

• **Democracy for America:** (*www.democracyforamerica.com/dfa-list.php*) Contribute, or recommend a candidate for endorsement.

• **Frontier PAC:** (*www.frontierpac.org*) Supports populist Democratic candidates in Western states.

These blogs also endorse candidates and report on key races:

• **Swing State Project** (*www.swingstateproject.com*)
• **Our Congress** (*www.ourcongress.org*)
• **Political Wire** (*www.politicalwire.com*)
• **Daily Kos** (*www.dailykos.com*)
• **MyDD** (*www.mydd.com*)

Web alert: Check out www.ombwatch.org. It promotes government accountability.

THE WAR ON PRIVACY

"Over the last five years under the Bush administration, Americans have experienced a full-scale assault on our rights to privacy. There have not only been over-the-top infringements under the guise of 'national security,' there have been corporate-backed efforts to eliminate financial privacy, and what seems to be anti-privacy moves based on partisan political motivations." —**David Sirota, www.davidsirota.com**

BOOK 'EM
The Patriot Act contains a provision that allows law enforcement agencies to secretly review your library records. However, the Bush administration has repeatedly insisted that this provision "has never been used to monitor what the public is reading and viewing."

They've been lying. In a 2002 survey of librarians, nearly half revealed that they were visited by "federal or local law enforcement agents demanding access to patron records." And in 2003, the University of Illinois released a study showing scores of libraries had been contacted by the Bush administration since the passage of the Patriot Act.

TAXING STORY
It's against the law for the IRS to disclose your tax information without your explicit consent...and for good reason: Your financial information is protected as "personal and private."

Nonetheless, when Congress passed a giant spending bill in 2004, Republicans inserted a last-minute provision that would have allowed them to legally examine anybody's income tax records. According to one Senator, "Any agent of the chairman of the Appropriations Committee [Note: obviously a Republican at the time] could go into IRS facilities anywhere in the country and get people's tax returns." That means anyone designated by the chairman, for any reason—personal or political—could examine your returns. Fortunately, the provision was discovered and ultimately withdrawn.

A CREDIT TO THE HOMELAND
In February 2006, according to the *Providence Journal* (RI), Walter Soehnge and his wife, Deana, decided to pay the balance on their MasterCard. "They sent in a large payment, a check for $6,522." After a

few days, they went online to make sure the payment had arrived.

It had, but their account still hadn't been credited. So they called and found out why: The amount they'd sent in was much larger than their normal monthly payment, so Homeland Security had to be notified...and Homeland Security had to give its okay before their money could be moved at all. Soehnge was appalled. "If it can happen to me," he said, "it can happen to [anyone]."

DOCTORING A PRESCRIPTION

In 2005, a 20-year-old Tucson, Arizona, woman was sexually assaulted. Her doctor issued a prescription for the Plan B emergency contraceptive pill to prevent pregnancy.

According to news reports: "She called dozens of pharmacies trying to fill the prescription and found most did not stock the drug. When she finally did find a pharmacy that stocked it, she was told the pharmacist on duty would not dispense it because of religious and moral objections.... 'I was so shocked,' said the woman...'I just did not understand how they could legally refuse to do this.... I just don't think this should be the pharmacist's decision.'"

JUST A REMINDER...

"The President last month admitted to ordering domestic spying operations without obtaining warrants as required by law," David Sirota wrote in January, 2006. "Bush has claimed the illegal operation only 'listens to a few [telephone] numbers' linked to al-Qaeda, even as the *Boston Globe* reported the Bush administration has 'been using computers to monitor all other Americans' international communications.' Bush still has yet to offer a satisfactory explanation as to why he has refused to seek warrants. Bonus: The story broke just after a string of stories about how the administration is having the FBI and Pentagon spy on anti-war, anti-poverty, and civil rights groups."

PARTY LINE

From the *Tampa Tribune*: "The Internal Revenue Service collected information on the political party affiliations of taxpayers in 20 states.... 'The bottom line is that we have never used this information,' said John Lipold, an IRS spokesman. 'There are strict laws in place that forbid it.'" Yeah? See "Book 'Em" on the previous page.

Congress didn't have time to read the Patriot Act before voting on it in 2001. (It passed 337 to 79.)

14. KNOW YOUR FOE

Q: *The Heritage Foundation, founded in 1973, was the first right-wing "think tank." Where did its start-up money come from?*
a) Selling beer b) A bake sale c) A dance marathon

BACKGROUND. Suppose you were guarding something precious, and knew someone was trying to take it away from you. You'd stand a better chance of defending it if you knew who they were, how they operated, and what tactics they might use.

Well, you *are* guarding something—American democracy.

So ask yourself: What do you really know about your foe?

EVERYONE SHOULD KNOW...

How the Radical Right took over America. It started with a 1971 memo proposing the creation of an infrastructure to support right-wing causes. After 30 years and a $3.5 billion investment, they've built it—right-wing think tanks, professorships, media, schools, judges, etc. This is *essential* information.

• The 1971 memo; the smoking gun of the "Vast Right-Wing Conspiracy": *www.mediatransparency.org/story.php?storyID=22*

• A short history, with some interesting links: *seetheforest.blogspot.com/2003_02_01_seetheforest_archive.html#903774839*

• An account from *Harper's* magazine, by Lewis Lapham. On the long side, but excellent. Print it out and read it offline. *www.mindfully.org/Reform/2004/Republican-Propaganda1sep04.htm*

The different factions of the "conservative" coalition. The Radical Right isn't a monolith; it's composed of different groups with different philosophies, from Libertarian to paleoconservative.

• A glossary: *rightweb.irc-online.org/charts/glossary.html*

• "Sectors of the Right": *www.publiceye.org/research/chart_of_sectors.html*

Groups and institutions that make up the Right. When you're familiar with names like the Bradley Foundation, Eagle Forum,

Answer: a) Heritage was founded with money donated by the Coors family.

and Rutherford Institute, you'll recognize their agenda and their connections to each other when you see them in the news.

• Great list: *rightweb.irc-online.org/profile/?sort=title_tagline#org*
• Another: *www.pfaw.org/go/right_wing_organizations*
• Foundations: *www.mediatransparency.org/funders.php*
• Direct links to right-wing groups: *www.publiceye.org/research/directories/dem_grp_undermine.html*

Who is the "Religious Right"? You can't make this stuff up. The Christian Reconstructionists may be the most dangerous anti-democratic force in America today.

• The Christian Reconstructionist movement: *www.publiceye .org/magazine/v08n1/chrisre2.html* or hear it from their own lips at *www.chalcedon.edu*

• And here are a few Christian Right Web sites: Family Research Council (*www.frc.org*), Focus on the Family (*www.family.org*), The Christian Coalition (*www.christiancoalition.org*)

• Track the Religious Right: (*www.talk2action.org*)

News slanted Right. How do right-wingers see the news? There are a number of news sites; these two will tell you all you need to know.

• World Net Daily: (*www.worldnetdaily.com*)
• NewsMax: (*www.newsmax.com*)

Right-wing bloggers. Here are three randomly selected blogs. If you can stand it, follow their links for more of the same.

• Free Republic: (*www.freerepublic.com*) Bloggers for whom the term "wing-nut" was invented.
• Right-Wing News (*www.rightwingnews.com*)
• Instapundit (*www.instapundit.com*) Most popular right-wing blog.

General sites: Excellent full-time coverage of the Radical Right.
• **Commonweal:** (*www.commonwealinstitute.org/information.html*)
• **Public Eye:** (*www.publiceye.org/articles/topics.php*)
• **Media Transparency:** (*www.mediatransparency.org*)

Strange bedfellows: The right-wing *Washington Times* is owned by the Moonies.

15. LEND US YOUR EARS

Al Franken, the high-profile author and Air America talk-show host, won one of the radio talk-show industry's most prestigious awards in 2005—the Freedom of Speech Award.

BACKGROUND. Who needs talk radio? Progressives do. It's a potent political weapon...and an essential part of the strategy to deliver our message to America.

The Right still rules the airwaves, but there are dozens of syndicated "lefty" talk-shows, and the number is growing. We even have our own radio network, Air America.

Want to help them? Radio's success (and power) is measured by the size of its audience. So...all you have to do is listen.

Think of it as a win-win-win proposition. You give progressive radio a few hours a week; they'll keep you entertained and informed; and together you'll strengthen the progressive movement.

BUILDING A MOVEMENT
How does talk radio make progressives stronger? A few examples:

• It gives us a chance to be heard...and to hear each other. "People need to...hear their opinions and beliefs shouted back at them," says political commentator Nicholas von Hoffman. "And they need to know that they are not alone."

• It gives us powerful new voices. Talk-show hosts like Ed Schultz, Randi Rhodes, Amy Goodman, Laura Flanders, and others are emerging as important spokespeople for the progressive cause.

• It reaches potential new voters. Example: For years, Rush Limbaugh's talk show was the only one aired on Armed Forces Radio. In 2005, because of liberal radio's growing presence, they agreed to air Ed Schultz as well. Soldiers can finally hear a progressive voice.

• It gives Democrats a home on the radio. "Republicans can always count on Limbaugh, Hannity, et al. to go out on the nation's air waves and organize support for conservative positions," notes media critic Robert Parry. Progressive radio gives Democrats the same benefit.

Survey results: More than 70% of the registered voters who listen to talk radio do actually vote.

SIMPLE THINGS YOU CAN DO
Find a show you like...and LISTEN.

• Even if you don't normally listen to talk radio, give it a shot. Be a part of the audience that makes progressive radio a success.

• If there's no liberal talk radio near you, try the Internet—Air America, Ed Schultz, Stephanie Miller, and the rest are online. Or try satellite radio; both Sirius and XM have progressive channels.

• Call in. Be a part of the program. One of the things that makes talk radio work is audience participation. It's a community.

Spread the word.

• Tell (or e-mail) your friends about it. They may not know about progressive talk radio or how to find it.

• Advertise to other drivers: Print a bumper sticker with the call letters of your local progressive station: e.g., "Listen to Air America on WCHL 1360 AM." (See page 52 for bumper sticker info).

Support them.

• Call local radio stations (both talk and music). Let them know you want to hear progressive or Democratic voices, and will patronize the advertisers who sponsor them.

• Write or e-mail current sponsors. Tell them you're listening and appreciate their support.

• Become an Air America Associate or a member of your local Pacifica radio station.

RESOURCES
These Web sites have links to every progressive talk show:

• *www.geocities.com/liberalprogressivetalk*

• *www.radiofreeamerica.info*

• *www.zianet.com/insightanalytical/radio.htm*

A few specific shows:

• Web connection to all Air America broadcasts: *www.airamericaradio.com*

• Ed Schultz, progressive radio's #1 host: *www.bigeddieradio.com*

• Amy Goodman and Juan Gonzalez: *www.democracynow.org*

• Stephanie Miller: *www.stephaniemiller.com*

16. PLAY TO WIN

According to recent studies, the most effective way to convince a voter to support your candidate is face-to-face contact. On average, at least 6.5% of the people you talk to (1 out of 15) will come around. That can be enough to swing an election.

BACKGROUND. If you were paying any attention at all during the last two presidential elections, you know that voter turnout played a big role in the results.

After Al Gore "lost" the 2000 election, Democrats vowed they wouldn't let a few errant votes make a difference again. They mobilized to get more of their voters to the polls in 2004…. But so did Karl Rove and the Republicans, who conducted two studies before the 2004 presidential election, and confirmed for themselves that

> people in politics should pay less attention to consultants, television advertising, polls, and "message," and more attention to the old-fashioned side of the business: registering voters, organizing volunteers, making face-to face contact during the last days of a campaign, and getting people to the polls on Election Day.

As a result, although the Democrats got a record number of votes in the 2004 presidential election, the Republicans did even better.

The point: For all the sophisticated techniques used in politics today, there's no substitute for knocking on doors, educating people, and providing rides to voters who need them. If we're serious about winning, this is where we have to put our efforts.

EVERY VOTE COUNTS…

In federal elections: In 2000 Al Gore lost Florida—and thus, the presidency—by 537 votes.

In state elections: The 2004 Washington gubernatorial election was the closest in the state's history. Out of 2.7 million votes cast, Christine Gregoire (D) defeated Dino Rossi (R) by 129 votes.

In local elections: In the 2005 city council race in Half Moon Bay, California, Bonnie Mcclung got 1,860 votes; Mike Ferreira got 1,845, a 15-vote margin. After a recount, it was cut to 8 votes.

Register to vote online: www.declareyourself.com

SIMPLE THINGS YOU CAN DO

Take care of voting at home. Make sure your family and all the progressives you know get to the polls for every election.

• "Vote for everything. No election is too small," says Carol Keyes, of People For the American Way. "People who are elected at lower levels today will move up to other offices and will be the ones who decide things like redistricting tomorrow."

• That means learning about every race on the ticket—which takes some work. (Check out alternative weeklies for candidate info.) It's worth the effort; studies show that most voters get "ballot fatigue" and leave some spots blank. If you share your research with friends, you can help them get through the whole ballot. E-mail them the info; ask them to forward it.

Get Out The Vote (GOTV). Volunteer to help a candidate you support (especially a local candidate), your local Democratic party, or work for a nonprofit progressive group, like ACORN, that canvasses for specific issues.

• GOTV tasks are simple. They include going door-to-door (leaving flyers and door hangers, or speaking to residents), and phone banking (calling and reminding people to vote). On Election Day, you might also help provide transportation for voters.

Think Ahead. It may seem like GOTV campaigns are the last thing to do before Election Day. Actually they start long before that. Here are three approaches to consider:

• **Adopt a Voter.** It's the last step in the process you began when you registered someone to vote (see p. 39). Follow up with your "adoptees." Make sure they know the issues, where their polling places are, have a sample ballot, and a ride to the polls.

• **Join a Voter Mobilization Group.** Help groups set up branches in your state, county, or town. Go to a leaders' training and learn to spearhead GOTV efforts during the next election:

    —America Votes (*www.americavotes.org*)

    —Project Vote (*www.projectvote.org*)

    —ACORN (*www.acorn.org*)

• **Help organize young voters.** See page 164 for info.

In 2004, nearly 1 out of every 11 voters skipped over their House race on the ballot.

THE FLYING SPAGHETTI MONSTER

*When you first read about the Christian Right's push to make "Intelligent Design" part of America's science education, what did you do? Bobby Henderson created "Pastafarianism," a new religion that challenged the Right and used satire to demonstrate just how preposterous their agenda is. In the process, he created a new cult hero—the Flying Spaghetti Monster. Now there's a book—*The Gospel of the Flying Spaghetti Monster*—and a Web site: www.venganza.org. Check it out. Here's a sample of Bobby's writing, from the Web.*

AN OPEN LETTER TO THE KANSAS SCHOOL BOARD:
I am writing you with much concern after having read of your hearing to decide whether the alternative theory of Intelligent Design should be taught along with the theory of Evolution. I think we can all agree that it is important for students to hear multiple viewpoints so they can choose for themselves the theory that makes the most sense to them. I am concerned, however, that students will only hear one theory of Intelligent Design.

Let us remember that there are multiple theories of Intelligent Design. I and many others around the world are of the strong belief that the universe was created by a Flying Spaghetti Monster. It was He who created all that we see and all that we feel. We feel strongly that the overwhelming scientific evidence pointing towards evolutionary processes is nothing but a coincidence, put in place by Him.

It is for this reason that I'm writing you today, to formally request that this alternative theory be taught in your schools, along with the other two theories. In fact, I will go so far as to say, if you do not agree to do this, we will be forced to proceed with legal action. I'm sure you see where we are coming from. If the Intelligent Design theory is not based on faith, but instead another scientific theory, as is claimed, then you must also allow our theory to be taught, as it is also based on science, not on faith.

"Pretty ironic that the only Republican with a prescription drug plan is Rush Limbaugh." —Jay Leno

Some find that hard to believe, so it may be helpful to tell you a little more about our beliefs. We have evidence that a Flying Spaghetti Monster created the universe. None of us, of course, were around to see it, but we have written accounts of it. We have several lengthy volumes explaining all details of His power. Also, you may be surprised to hear that there are over 10 million of us, and growing. We tend to be very secretive, as many people claim our beliefs are not substantiated by observable evidence. What these people don't understand is that He built the world to make us think the earth is older than it really is. For example, a scientist may perform a carbon-dating process on an artifact. He finds that approximately 75% of the Carbon-14 has decayed by electron emission to Nitrogen-14, and infers that this artifact is approximately 10,000 years old, as the half-life of Carbon-14 appears to be 5,730 years. But what our scientist does not realize is that every time he makes a measurement, the Flying Spaghetti Monster is there changing the results with His Noodly Appendage. We have numerous texts that describe in detail how this can be possible and the reasons why He does this. He is of course invisible and can pass through normal matter with ease.

I'm sure you now realize how important it is that your students are taught this alternate theory. It is absolutely imperative that they realize that observable evidence is at the discretion of a Flying Spaghetti Monster. Furthermore, it is disrespectful to teach our beliefs without wearing His chosen outfit, which of course is full pirate regalia. I cannot stress the importance of this enough, and unfortunately cannot describe in detail why this must be done as I fear this letter is already becoming too long. The concise explanation is that He becomes angry if we don't.

You may be interested to know that global warming, earthquakes, hurricanes, and other natural disasters are a direct effect of the shrinking numbers of Pirates since the 1800s…. There is a statistically significant inverse relationship between pirates and global temperature.

In conclusion, thank you for taking the time to hear our views and beliefs. I hope I was able to convey the importance of teaching this theory to your students. We will of course be able to train the teachers in this alternate theory. I am eagerly awaiting your response, and hope dearly that no legal action will need to be taken. I think we can all look forward to the time when these three theories are given equal time in our science classrooms across the country, and eventually the world; One third time for Intelligent Design, one third time for Flying Spaghetti Monsterism, and one third time for logical conjecture based on overwhelming observable evidence.

Sincerely Yours,

Bobby Henderson, concerned citizen.

*　　*　　*　　*

QUIZ:
WHO SAID IT?

Match the quote to the famous Republican who reportedly said it.

1. "I AM the federal law!"

2. "You've done a nice job of decorating the White House" (to then-Secretary of the Interior Gale Norton).

3. "I think that gay marriage is something that should be between a man and a woman."

4. "Capital punishment is our society's recognition of the sanctity of human life."

5. "Africa is a nation with a lot of diseases."

a) Governor Arnold Schwarzenegger

b) Celebrity Jessica Simpson

c) Sen. Orrin Hatch (R-UT)

d) President George W. Bush

e) Then-Majority Leader, now indicted ex-Majority Leader, Rep. Tom DeLay (R-TX)

Answers: 1-e, 2-b, 3-a, 4-c, 5-d

Ben Cohen, co-founder of Ben & Jerry's Ice Cream, also founded True Majority (www.truemajority.org)

IT TAKES

AN EFFORT

17. ADOPT A BLOG

According to December 2005 figures, the Left's Daily Kos (called "the most important force in the blogosphere" by the right-wing Weekly Standard*) gets more than 640,000 page views a day. Its closest competitor, the Right's Instapundit, gets about 144,000.*

BACKGROUND. It's amazing to see how the Left has taken over the "blogosphere." For years, there was no place progressives could make themselves heard—the mainstream media either ignored them or fatally watered down every argument with their "he said, she said" reporting.

But now, because of political blogs, progressive voices are regaining their influence in America. Are you reading them yet?

WELCOME TO THE BLOGOSPHERE

• Blog is short for "Web log," an online journal meant for the public. It can be about anything—from fashion to politics.

• Progressive blogs contain some of the most interesting and entertaining political commentary being written anywhere. They're updated constantly…and if you get tired of one, there are literally hundreds more to check out.

• Blogs vary in tone: Some are sarcastic, some are defiantly partisan, some are straight reporting. Content varies, too—from opinion and commentary to video clips to muckraking.

• Most are interactive. Readers get to post comments, ask questions, and observe others doing the same. It's an inclusive process that builds a sense of community. You'll also find "links" to other sites, so you can hop from blog to blog.

• We've listed a few of the more established progressive blogs on the next page (and throughout the book). Start with these, then follow the links on each site until you find ones that appeal to you.

SIMPLE THINGS YOU CAN DO

Adopt the ones you like.

• Remember, these blogs are a vital component of the progressive infrastructure. Your role in strengthening and supporting them

More than half of U.S. reporters believe that blogs have made journalists more accountable.

makes you a valuable resource as well.

• By increasing traffic on a blog, you (1) help get their message out *and* (2) support them financially. Ad rates are determined by the number of "hits," or visits, a Web site gets, so ad revenue increases as the number of viewers grows.

• Be their PR rep. Spread their name around: E-mail their articles to friends and suggest that they check out the sites themselves, or send out lists of favorite blogs. You'll be surprised how many people don't know where to start with blogs.

• Make a donation. Most bloggers have day jobs, and put out their own money to keep their Web sites open. A small donation may make a big difference to them. Many also sell T-shirts, mugs, etc.

RESOURCES

• **Lefty Blogs** (*www.leftyblogs.com*). Lists all the latest postings from more than 2,000 progressive blogs.

• **The Liberal Blog Advertising Network** (*www.blogads.com/advertise/liberal_blog_advertising_network/order*). Lists 80+ blogs, links.

• Read the definitive article/study: ***The Emergence of the Progressive Blogosphere*** (*www.ndnpac.org/npi/blogreport.html*).

20 Blogs We Like

Americablog (*Americablog.com*)

Booman Tribune (*www.boomantribune.com*)

BOPnews (*www.bopnews.com*)

Brad Blog (*www.bradblog.com*)

Carpetbagger Report (*www.thecarpetbaggerreport.com*)

Crooks and Liars (*www.crooksandliars.com*)

Daily Kos (*www.dailykos.com*)

Daou Report (*daoureport.salon.com/default.aspx*)

Eschaton (*atrios.blogspot.com*)

Firedoglake (*www.firedoglake.com*)

Huffington Post (*www.huffingtonpost.com*)

Hullabaloo (*digbysblog.blogspot.com*)

The Left Coaster (*theleftcoaster.com*)

MyDD (*www.mydd.com*)

Political Animal (*www.washingtonmonthly.com*)

Political Wire (*politicalwire.com*)

T Bogg (*tbogg.blogspot.com*)

Talking Points Memo (*talkingpointsmemo.com*)

TalkLeft (*talkleft.com*)

TAPPED (*www.prospect.org/weblog*)

This Modern World (*www.thismodernworld.com*)

A WOMAN'S PLACE

There are plenty of politically active women aligned with the Radical Right…and statements like these really make you wonder why.

The feminist agenda is not about equal rights for women. It is about a socialist, antifamily political movement that encourages women to leave their husbands, kill their children, practice witchcraft, destroy capitalism, and become lesbians."

—**Rev. Pat Robertson,** *The 700 Club*

"[Pro-choice activists] are usually pretty big, heavyset women who look like they've been over working Oktoberfest for the last six years. You know, there's six beer mugs in each arm. All right, it's a stereotype, but I swear looking at that footage, that's what you see—a lot of people who are angry, women who have shed their femininity and adopted a masculine outlook, and are fiercely protective of abortion, which is the holy sacrament of feminism."

—**Robert H. Knight,** *The Family Research Council*

"Rail as they will about 'discrimination,' women are simply not endowed by nature with the same measures of single-minded ambition and the will to succeed in the fiercely competitive world of Western capitalism."

—**Pat Buchanan,** *conservative columnist*

"Women have babies and men provide the support. If you don't like the way we're made you've got to take it up with God."

—**Phyllis Schlafly,** *The Eagle Forum*

"Most of these feminists are radical, frustrated lesbians, many of them, and man-haters, and failures in their relationships with men, and who have declared war on the male gender. The biblical condemnation of feminism has to do with its radical philosophy and goals. That's the bottom line."

—**Rev. Jerry Falwell**

"There are so many women on the floor of Congress, it looks like a mall." —Rep. Henry Hyde (R-IL)

18. WRITE ON

In 2005, MoveOn.org encouraged its members to write to local newspapers and support saving the filibuster in the Senate. The result: They reached millions of people with their message. About 60,000 letters were sent; about 12,000 of them were published.

BACKGROUND. Want to see a progressive message in your local newspaper? Write it yourself: Send a letter to the editor or compose an op-ed piece. It's worth the effort; believe it or not, more people read the letters to the editor than any other section of the paper, except the front page.

By speaking up, you'll also provide a counterbalance to the Radical Right, who've been using the power of this community bulletin board for years. Some radical Christian groups have even created *letter-writing teams* to flood newspapers with their opinions. Now it's time for us to "write back."

DON'T UNDERESTIMATE YOUR POWER

• *You can influence your neighbors.* "Letters to the editor probably have the most bang for your buck of any [message] delivery system there is, because the people who read them are friends and neighbors," says Benjamin Branzel of MoveOn.org "No other form of political communication is as personalized and effective."

• *You can influence local, state, even national policy.* Most people don't realize that politicians have their staffs monitor letters sections to gauge local opinion. Particularly interesting letters often get passed on to them personally. (Hint: If you really want to be sure a politician sees your letter, mention him or her by name.)

• *You can influence editorial decisions...even if your letter's not printed.* Editors often use letters to evaluate which topics to cover in future articles or editorials. The more letters a newspaper gets on a certain topic, the more attention they'll pay to it in the future.

• *You make other voices stronger.* "If media outlets get letters from a dozen people raising the same issue," explains FAIR Media, "they'll most likely publish one or two of them. So even if your letter doesn't get into print, it may help another one with a similar point of view get published."

Experts say: A shorter letter has a better chance of being read. Why? People read short letters first.

SIMPLE THINGS YOU CAN DO

Write a letter (150–200 words): See Resources below for tips on composing letters for publication.

• Don't wait until something gets you upset; write regularly—say, once a month. If you're looking for a good topic, check out right-wing Web sites to see what *they're* up in arms about. Or write about one of the subjects in this book.

• Not every letter has to be for publication. If a specific reporter does something noticeable (good or bad), send a personal note.

• Many papers have an ombudsman, or public editor. If you want to criticize or compliment the paper itself, you can write to them.

• Remember: Every publication's guidelines are unique. Find addresses and rules on the editorial/opinion page, or their Web site.

Write an op-ed: It's longer than a letter (usually 600–800 words) and there's more competition for space. You may want to call the paper for length requirements.

• See the FAIR Web site for tips on writing op-eds.

Send in your piece: Personnel and addresses are usually inside the front page, on the editorial page, or on the paper's Web site.

• Most newspapers prefer e-mail to regular mail.

• Send letters to weekly community newspapers, too. The smaller the circulation, the easier it is to get your letter printed.

• Don't forget newspapers targeted to specific audiences; e.g., Hispanic or African American papers, and denominational papers.

RESOURCES

• **20/20 Vision.** Excellent instructions on letters to the editor. (*www.2020vision.org/resources/r_activists.htm#lte*)

• **FAIR (Fairness and Accuracy in Reporting).** Tips for writing letters and op-eds. (*www.fair.org/index.php?page=122*)

• **Garbl's Writing Center.** Links to other letter-writing sites. (*home.comcast.net/~garbl/writing/action.htm#editor*)

• **Sierra Club.** Tips and newspaper links. (*www.sierraclub.org/takeaction/toolkit/letters.asp*)

• **New Voyager.** Lists and links to newspapers across the country, including local papers. (*www.newspaperlinks.com/home.cfm*)

THE WAR ON PUBLIC HEALTH

It's disturbing that people who consider themselves "pro-life" consistently side with forces that are willing to endanger people's health to make a few dollars...or that they choose ideological purity over genuine concern for people's well-being. There are literally hundreds of examples of right-wing disregard for public health. Here a few.

POISON PEN
More than 10,000 children ingest rat poison every year. That's why, in 1998, Clinton's EPA required rat poison manufacturers to 1) add a bittering agent to discourage kids from eating it, and 2) a dye to make it obvious if a child already had.

But in 2001, right after Bush took office, the EPA reversed the requirement at the industry's request. Their justification: It "would make the poison less attractive to rats and could damage household property." Fortunately, in 2005, a judge overruled them, saying they had acted without a "scintilla of evidence."

CONDOM-NATION

The Centers for Disease Control (CDC), part of the U.S. Department of Health and Human Services, is supposed to base policy decisions on "protecting the health and safety of all Americans." Since condoms are 98-100% effective in preventing pregnancy and sexually transmitted infections (including HIV), the CDC Web site recommended that sexually active people use them.

But in 2002, at the urging of the Christian Right, the CDC Web fact sheet on condoms was changed so it had *no information on condoms* at all. It read: "The surest way to avoid transmission of sexually transmitted diseases is to abstain from sexual intercourse, or to be in a long-term mutually monogamous relationship." A CDC official commented, "This is really...endangering people's lives." (It has since been changed back).

In October 2002, the Bush administration issued regulations making fetuses, but not...

PLYING THEIR TRADE

Formaldehyde is a chemical used in plywood manufacturing. It's also a known toxin and pollutant, subject to EPA regulations. "In addition to causing nausea and eye, throat, and skin irritation," reports the Natural Resources Defense Council, "exposure to the chemical can cause leukemia in humans."

In 2004, EPA officials with previous ties to the timber and chemical industries helped plywood manufacturers get the "safe" level of formaldehyde increased...by *10,000 times*. It saved the industry $66 million, and put workers in plywood factories at risk. "The formaldehyde fix was in at the EPA," said John Walke, director of NRDC's Clean Air Program. "The Bush administration pushed aside scientifically supported health concerns to weaken safeguards that will protect the plywood industry's profits."

MERCURY SINKING

Mercury is a toxic chemical that pollutes water, soil, and air, contaminates the food chain, and threatens human health. Because about 40% of the human-caused mercury in the environment comes from coal-burning electric power plants, President Clinton's EPA ruled that mercury emissions from coal plants should be reduced 90% by 2008.

However, in a deal with the power industry, President George W. Bush—through his so-called "Clear Skies" proposal—has allowed mercury emissions to actually increase, effectively overriding a key provision of the Clean Air Act. White House staffers even edited EPA reports to downplay Mercury's health hazards. One passage originally read:

> "Recent published studies have shown an association between methylmercury exposure and an increased risk of heart attacks and coronary disease in adult men."

It was changed to:

> "It has been hypothesized that there is an association between methylmercury exposure and an increased risk of coronary disease; however this warrants further study as the new studies currently available present conflicting results."

...pregnant women, eligible for health care under the State Children's Health Insurance Program.

19. PRACTICE RANDOM ACTS OF PATRIOTISM

*"I never use the words 'Democrats' and 'Republicans.'
It's liberals and Americans." —James Watt, Ronald
Reagan's Secretary of the Interior (1981–83)*

BACKGROUND. If you're a patriot and a progressive, you should be angry. The Right has done its best to steal something precious from you—your birthright as an American. They've wrapped themselves in *our* flag and claimed it for themselves. They've tried to take *our* national anthem, *our* Constitution. The worst thing is that to a large extent they've succeeded. Many progressives are reluctant to identify with traditional American symbols now because they seem so...well...*right-wing*.

Progressive values are true American values. It's time we stopped doubting it...and started experiencing it.

WHO'S A PATRIOT?
Patriotism wasn't invented by ultraconservatives.

• The Pledge of Allegiance was written by a Christian socialist named Francis Bellamy. He said that when he wrote "one nation indivisible, with liberty and justice for all," he had corporate robber barons and oppressed workers in mind.

• "This Land is Your Land" was written by Woody Guthrie, a progressive who wrote thousands of protest songs and wrote a regular column for *The People's Weekly*.

• The Statue of Liberty's famous inscription ("Give me your tired, your poor/Your huddled masses yearning to breathe free...") was penned by progressive poet Emma Lazarus, expressing a leftist political message that challenged the typical anti-poor, racist, anti-immigrant sentiments of the time.

• "America, the Beautiful" was written by Katherine Lee Bates, a professor at Wellesley College who was deeply involved in women's suffrage, feminism, poverty, and worker's rights. She published her lyrics in a small book that included poems of outrage about Ameri-

About half the American flags sold in the U.S. are made in China.

ca's war to conquer the Philippines. Her life partner was economist Katherine Coman, another activist.

SIMPLE THINGS YOU CAN DO

Practice Random Acts of Patriotism. Think of these as exercise. Repetition builds strength—in this case, a stronger identity as an American. When you take your patriotism seriously, others will, too.

You can...

• Learn the national anthem and sing it at public events. It's your song. Note: Two-thirds of U.S. adults don't know all the words. There's an initiative to teach the lyrics, called the National Anthem Project. Check it out: *www.tnap.org*

• Wear the stars and stripes. Back in the 1960s, when counterculture hero Abbie Hoffman did it, the Right called it blasphemous. Times change: Now they call it fashion. As Abbie proved, wearing a piece of America is a way to claim it.

• Get some friends or your group together and sponsor a float in your local Memorial Day or 4th of July parades. Pick a patriotic theme and a powerful progressive message, like "Equal Opportunity for All" or "Save the Wilderness."

• Read the Constitution. Knowing what's in the document enables you to understand the American ideal and act in its behalf. Patriotism *is* upholding the Constitution.

• Don't forget the Declaration of Independence. It's a beacon of hope. America was created by dreamers who believed in a "more perfect union"; as progressives, we benefit from their inspiration, wisdom, and example.

Or practice your own act of patriotism:

• "Whenever I see the names of soldiers who have died," a staunchly progressive friend confides, "I stop and observe a moment of respect. When their pictures are shown on TV, I make sure to really look at their faces, and read their names and where they're from. I stop whatever else I may be doing, and stand or sit quietly in front of the images. Lately, because the lists are so long, I've taken to singing 'America, the Beautiful' out loud. It just seems like the right thing to do."

To read the U.S. Constitution: *www.usconstitution.net/const.html*

REAL PATRIOTISM...

Inspiring thoughts that remind us of our responsibility as citizens.

"We must not confuse dissent with disloyalty. When the loyal opposition dies, I think the soul of America dies with it."

—**Edward R. Murrow**

"Men in authority will always think criticism of their policies is dangerous. They'll always equate their policies with patriotism, and find criticism subversive."

—**Henry Steele Commager**

"I love America more than any other country in this world, and, exactly for this reason, I insist on the right to criticize her perpetually."

—**James Baldwin**

"Moral cowardice that keeps us from speaking our minds is as dangerous to this country as irresponsible talk. The right way is not always the popular and easy way. Standing for right when it is unpopular is a true test of moral character."

—**Sen. Margaret Chase Smith**

"If you want a symbolic gesture, don't burn the flag; wash it."

—**Norman Thomas**

"Each man must for himself alone decide what is right and what is wrong, which course is patriotic and which isn't. You cannot shirk this and be a man. To decide against your conviction is to be an unqualified and excusable traitor, both to yourself and to your country, let them label you as they may."

—**Mark Twain**

"To announce that there must be no criticism of the president, or that we are to stand by the president, right or wrong, is not only unpatriotic and servile, but is morally treasonable to the American public."

—**Theodore Roosevelt**

"Restriction of free thought and free speech is the most dangerous of all subversions. It is the one un-American act that could most easily defeat us."

—**Justice William O. Douglas**

"There are those, I know, who will say that the liberation of humanity, the freedom of man and mind, is nothing but a dream. They are right. It is the American dream."

—**Archibald MacLeish**

20. TAKE BACK THE CHURCHES

There are about 500,000 churches, temples, and mosques in the USA; in any given month, about 60% of Americans attend them.

BACKGROUND. Religious institutions have an enormous impact on American politics. "If you want to know why conservatives control America, look no further than the churches," contends Rev. Erik Thorson, a Lutheran pastor who was forced to resign his ministries in rural Montana after he preached against war. "The great secret of the American debate is that most...political opinions don't get formed by FOX News or Rush Limbaugh—the world view that is closest to the heart of most conservative Americans is formed on Sunday morning at worship, and at weekly Bible studies."

If you go to church or temple (or plan to), you have a critical role to play in the fight against the Right. By becoming active in your congregation and standing up for your liberal faith and values, you help restore—or strengthen—a progressive presence in one of our most influential institutions.

CONSERVATIVE OR LIBERAL?

Should you go to a progressive congregation because you agree with its politics, or a conservative one so you can add some progressive thinking?

• "Go to a place that's comfortable and spiritually moving to you," suggests Dr. Douglas Ottati of the Union Theological Seminary in Richmond, Virginia. "Show up, worship there, and give them money. But bring your philosophy to church with you. Talk to members of your religious community about how your political and religious beliefs connect."

• Wherever you go, Thorson says, "be visible in worship. Park your car with the Kerry/Edwards bumper sticker in the church parking lot. Speak up at Bible studies and challenge the persons who try to trumpet the FOX News talking points as if they relate to the texts. Let the pastors and priests know that you are there to back them up when they challenge corporatism, welfare cuts,

"The Christian Right always throws around this term 'the liberal elite.' I keep thinking to myself...

bigotry...war fever. Read *God's Politics*, by Jim Wallis, and lend it to other friends who profess Christian faith."

• "Some people feel it's their mission to bring a progressive voice to a conservative church. That's a worthy goal. But it takes a very strong person to do this," says Rev. Brad Bunnin of Berkeley, California.

• Robert Chase of the United Church of Christ adds, "Sometimes, the entrenchment of conservative views in a church is so profound that progressives wind up fighting frustrating battles for years. They may get disillusioned and leave, or they may even be asked to leave. If you're not sure where to go, join with other progressives in a congregation...and *then* engage conservatives. Don't try to fight that battle alone."

PRACTICALLY SPEAKING
When you become a member of a congregation, you also get...

• **Access to their facilities.** Members of most churches and temples can use the social/parish hall, kitchen, meeting rooms, parking lot, etc., for groups they belong to. Organizing to stop Wal-Mart from coming into the neighborhood? Have forums at the social hall. Having a craft fair to raise money for our troops? Hold it on the lawn at the church.

• **Credibility.** Holding an event at a respected religious institution can give event organizers instant credibility. And on a personal level, being able to say "We talked about that at church," can be a way to seize the moral high ground in any conversation.

• **A forum.** "You can put things in the Church bulletin, speak up on Sunday when announcements are called for, and put things up on the bulletin board," says Shannon Lee. "Church is a great place to engage neighbors about causes that affect them and their world."

RESOURCES
Many religious institutions now have Web sites. So you can Google religious groups—use keywords like "welcome," "justice," and "diversity" along with "church," "synagogue," or "mosque"—to find a progressive congregation. Then go check it out.

For more religious resources, see page 86.

THE RELIGIOUS LEFT

To fight the Religious Right, we need a Religious Left. You can find some organizations listed on pages 154 and 160. Here's an additional listing of groups that bring religion and progressive politics together.

The Sojourners. (*www.sojo.net*) Progressive evangelicals led by Jim Wallis. "A movement of spirituality and social change."

Network of Spiritual Progressives (*www.spiritualprogressives.org*) Activists led by Rabbi Michael Lerner.

The Revealer (*www.therevealer.org*) "A daily review of religion in the news, dedicated to free speech as a first principle."

Theocracywatch (*www.theocracywatch.org*) "Raises awareness about the pervasive role of the Religious Right in the U.S. government."

Texas Freedom Network (*www.tfn.org*) Includes material on separation of church and state, Bible interpretation, and the Texas Faith Network.

The Interfaith Alliance (*www.interfaithalliance.org*) "Faith-based voice countering the Radical Right and promoting religion's positive role." In January 2006, launched "State of Belief," a Sunday radio show, with Air America.

Talk To Action (*www.talk2action.org*) Learn about the Religious Right and what to do about it. Frederick Clarkson is co-founder.

Unitarian Universalists (*www.uua.org*). The UU's are longterm progressive activists.

United Church of Christ (*www.ucc.org*). Descended from the Pilgrims' religious community. Has a staunchly liberal view of theology.

Evangelical Environmental Network (*creationcare.org*) Believe the environment is a moral issue. Also: *www.whatwouldjesusdrive.org*

www.Streetprophets.com. A religious blog from Dailykos.

Wisdom University (*www.wisdomuniversity.org/sacred-activism-conference.html*)

"HERE'S WHAT *I* DO..."

*More testimonials from the hundreds of grassroots
activists who sent us their ideas for this book.*

I NEVER ENTER A BAR that has FOX Network on without asking them to please turn to any other channel. When challenged, I say any channel is fine, I just don't feel it is appropriate to ask all customers to watch right-wing Republican TV. If they refuse, I walk. I've only had to walk about 1/3 of the time. I believe all challenges—even when I wind up leaving—are victories. Twice, I've talked to the manager and let him know that I often come to his place, but since he won't change channels—again, any channel—I am forced to e-mail every Democrat I know to ask them not to patronize his bar."

—**Wade Dokken, Montana**

"HERE'S MY SUGGESTION: Make a simple information sheet that provides clearly stated, solid facts about (for example) the Iraq war, Social Security, evolution, etc. Add a few trustworthy Web sites. Slip them into magazines in waiting rooms, newspapers, tuck them under your check in a restaurant, hand them out at street corners, mail stacks of them to friends.

I've done this twice. I've heard stories of the cards finding their way into people's hands all over the country. It's satisfying to leave a doctor's waiting room knowing that the next person who picks up *People* magazine, or whatever, will—at the very least—have a few moments when they confront some important questions."

—**J. Salas, New York**

"PUT UP A LAWN SIGN! Everytime I've canvassed, I've found plenty of voters who agree with the progressive candidate, but stay quiet because they're surrounded by more vocal neighbors with various right-wing signs ("Vote Pro-Life," "Vote [insert conservative here]"). People sometimes feel more comfortable expressing themselves if there is strength in numbers—with one lawn sign, you may discover people on your block you never realized felt the same way!"

—**Lois Godach, Ohio**

21. IT'S A FRAME

"Tax relief, tort reform, partial birth abortion, death tax, marriage penalty. You've heard them all before....You've probably even used the terms yourself. And each time you did, you were helping to legitimize the Republicans' views on the issues." —**Tom Ball, Political Cortex**

BACKGROUND. Have you ever wanted to have X-ray vision, like Superman, so you could see through walls? George Lakoff's book *Don't Think of an Elephant*, is like X-ray vision for progressives. It enables us to see through the opaque language that the Radical Right uses to wield power and control, and discover what's hidden behind it.

For a long time, we wondered why the Right's messages always sounded clearer and smarter than ours. It turns out there's a method behind their success.... And the method is called *framing*.

WHAT IS FRAMING?

• Each of us has our own way of looking at the world—we see things as good or bad, valuable or worthless, right or wrong, etc. That world-view is embedded in everything we say and think.

• If you hear the word "family," for example, you instantly get a whole set of feelings, ideas, and images.

• It's amazing how much information one word can contain. It *frames* your whole understanding of a complex set of concepts and experiences. We all think this way—i.e., in frames.

• This idea—long understood by linguists—has now made its way into politics. Republicans, Lakoff tells us, have invested millions of dollars over a long period of time, to develop and master the art of *framing* to present their policies to the public.

THE POLITICS OF FRAMING

In his book, Lakoff uses the term "tax relief" to illustrate how they do it: As soon as Bush was elected, he says, "the phrase 'tax relief' began coming out of the White House." The newpapers picked it up as if it were a neutral term." Soon all the media—and even

Republican messaging: "Never say 'Foreign Trade.' Instead, say 'International Trade.'"

Democrats—were using it to describe Bush's tax-cut programs.

But the phrase isn't neutral. It's a Trojan Horse that carries a specific pro-Republican, anti-Democrat message. "For there to be relief," Lakoff explains, "there must be an affliction (taxes), an afflicted party (the American people), and someone who removes the afflictions (the Republicans)—and is therefore a hero. When you add 'tax' to 'relief' you get a metaphor that taxation is an affliction, and anybody against relieving this affliction (Democrats/liberals) is a villain...Every time the phrase tax relief is used, this view of taxation as an affliction, and of conservatives as heroes, gets reinforced."

• "This is what framing is about," Lakoff says—finding language that communicates your world view. But significantly, framing isn't just about words. Lakoff makes it very clear that people must have a deep understanding of their own ideas, beliefs and value systems first. Then "the frames follow." He says: "It's not just language—the ideas are primary. The language carries and evokes those ideas."

SIMPLE THINGS YOU CAN DO

• First and foremost, this process requires that you understand your own values and beliefs. (See Ground Rule #1, page 16.) Again, ideas come first. "The frames will follow."

• Read *Don't Think of an Elephant*. It's a great intro to the concept

• Learn to recognize right-wing frames—don't just accept ideas the way they're presented. Then learn to reframe, or restate an idea in your own way. Arguing against someone's frame only reinforces it.

• Don't expect to learn this overnight—it takes work. But it's worth the effort.

RESOURCES

• **Rockridge Institute** (*www.rockridgeinstitute.org*): Lakoff's group.
• **Political Cortex** (*www.politicalcortex.com/keyword/framing*)
• **DemSpeak** (*www.demspeak.com*)
• **Frameshop** (*www.frameshopisopen.com*)
• **Frameworks Institute** (*www.frameworksinstitute.org*)
• **The Metaphor Project**
(*www.cointelligence.org/metaphorproject.html*)

Watch out for framing pitfalls: Read this blog post and its comments: *www.alternet.org/story/31318s*

22. "BOOK 'EM"

According to the American Library Association (ALA), despite severe budget cuts, libraries are being used more than ever. There were an estimated 1.3 billion visits to U.S. public libraries in 2004.

BACKGROUND. You probably don't think of supporting a public library as a political act. That's because most of us take our libraries—and the free access to information they provide—for granted.

But to many on the Religious Right, libraries are a beachhead in the culture wars. Each time they successfully censor a book or intimidate a librarian, they move one step closer to dictating community standards for all of us.

If you value free speech and an informed public, libraries are worth fighting for.

BANNED AIDS

Book Notes. The ALA estimates that there are over 500 attempts to ban books in school and public libraries every year. Usual reasons: sex, profanity. But anything goes: Some parents object to kids' books with "too many rainbows." The reason: "Rainbows are considered a sign of 'New Age' religiosity."

• Since 1990, libraries have reportedly received more complaints about Harry Potter than any other series. Why? It's "pro-witchcraft." In 2002, a New Mexico minister actually held a Harry Potter book-burning.

• Sign of things to come? In 2005, "Republican state Rep. Gerald Allen of Alabama introduced a bill to bar public school libraries from stocking books written by gay authors or about gay characters." This would mean no Plato, no Socrates, no Walt Whitman.

Sneak Attacks. The Right's strategy of "starving the beast"—creating deficits to undermine funding for social services—has devastated libraries. In 2005, nearly $85 million was cut from library budgets. Some libraries have been forced to reduce their hours and staff; some have closed altogether.

A favorite target of right-wing library censors: Books by "young adult" author Judy Blume.

SIMPLE THINGS YOU CAN DO

Library Politics

• *Create an informal alliance with a librarian.* Have them contact you if the Right attacks. Start a list of people who'll join you, and be ready to mobilize your group to fight back.

• *Learn how to lobby.* Take a lesson from "Family-Friendly Libraries," an offshoot of the Radical Right's Focus on the Family. Hold your nose and check out *www.fflibraries.org*

• *Support Banned Books Week.* Each year since 1982, the ALA and other groups have sponsored Banned Books Week to keep freedom of speech in public view. Many libraries have special displays, but not all. Call yours—ask what they're doing and if you can help. If they're too timid, get a local bookstore to take it on.

• *Turn library issues into political issues.* Smoke out the Right: Get local and state candidates to go on record with their views on library freedom and funding.

Donate Materials. Some right-wingers steal books they disapprove of. Help replace them. Ask at the library.

• Volunteer to raise money…or donate some. Libraries accept cash.

Join the Friends of the Library. Most libraries have a Friends of the Library (FOL) to help raise money, supply volunteers, etc. Make a political statement and join them. It's a minimal commitment, and it makes your library stronger to have people like you involved.

RESOURCES

• **The American Library Association:** *www.ala.org* or 1-800-545-2433. A comprehensive Web site with articles, resources, and ideas for action.

• **The Friends of the Library USA:** *www.folusa.org* or 1-800-9FOLUSA (1-800-936-5872). Supports local Friends of the Library groups. Web site will direct you to the nearest FOL.

• **Library Blogs:** There are numerous blogs about libraries and library advocacy. Check them out with the directory at: *www.libdex.com/weblogs.html*

Americans go to libraries more than twice as often as they go to the movies.

23. SOCIAL-ISM

Drinking Liberally, "an informal, Democratic drinking club where socializing and politics mix," started in New York City in 2003. It's becoming a political force itself—there are now more than 120 chapters around the USA, with new ones forming every week.

BACKGROUND. Who says building a political movement has to be hard work? You can do it while you're knitting. Or while you're talking about books. Or at a bar. All it takes is a group of people who share your point of view and can have a good time together.

Don't underestimate the power of social connection in building a movement. The more you enjoy being in the company of your political allies, the stronger that connection will become. Every time people gather, there's an opportunity to strengthen the progressive community.

GETTING TOGETHER
Some ways people have combined their political and social lives:
• "I've started holding 'Progressive Parties' to bond with other people, identify like minds, talk about issues, and build a community that will be supportive and ready for action," writes Dean Roberts. "I find this activity particularly helpful. It's not just about 'preaching to the converted'—it's about knowing where to turn when it's time to act. Plus, there's something to be said for feeling 'strength in numbers.'"
• "When it comes to letter writing, one of the best ideas I've come across is from the Quakers," says Greg Small. "They have a lunchtime group meeting where folks are provided with brief information on a specific issue, as well as writing tools, so they can write a letter and have it posted before they leave. It's easy to adapt this to progressive issues. If you do it on a regular basis, people get to know each other and can be activists in other ways, too."
• From the Drinking Liberally Web site: "In the weeks following the November 2004 election, liberals needed a drink...and they

needed a place where the grassroots energy of the past 18 months could continue. Drinking Liberally was the answer. It's an easy first step for political involvement because Drinking Liberally's weekly guests and regulars include local politicians and their staffers, political organizers, activists, would-be volunteers, and newly interested chitchatters—all in a casual, inclusive environment."

• "I host a book club that reads progressive nonfiction books," says Deborah Steele. "We have monthly or bimonthly discussions. It's a chance to learn, and to strengthen bonds with people whose point of view you share."

• A yarn shop in Grant's Pass, Oregon, reportedly has liberal and conservative knitting groups (on different days, of course). Bad news: The city is largely Republican, so the "conservative day" attracts a lot more people.

• Meetup.com was inspired by Harvard sociologist Robert Putnam's book *Bowling Alone*. "The premise of the book is that, over the past 50 years, dramatically fewer Americans participate in community events, from PTA meetings to bowling leagues." Meetup's founders wanted to try to help people connect more frequently. Now Meetup is being used as a political mobilizing tool. (See page 94.)

SIMPLE THINGS YOU CAN DO

Ready to start your own group? Here's what you can do:

• **Start a chapter of Drinking Liberally.** (*www.drinkingliberally.org*) Complete instructions are on their Web site.

• **Sponsor a letter-writing party.** People For the American Way have info on their site (*www.fcnl.org/getin/resources/letter_writing .htm*) or just Google "letter-writing party."

• **Start a progressive book group.** Get your inspiration from TPM Cafe Book Club (*bookclub.tpmcafe.com*). Get guidelines from: *progressivebookclubs.blogspot.com*

• **Start a progressive knitting group.** How to start a "stitch 'n' bitch" group—for progressives: (*www.stitchnbitchla.com*)

• **Come up with your own social group.** Give it a progressive slant. Anything works—art, music, sports, etc.

For inspiration, check out The Ruth Group: (*www.ruthgroup.org*)

"HERE'S WHAT *I* DO…"

Nancy Cunningham is an inspiration. After the 2004 election, the energetic Texan created a community of progressives who support each other politically…and have a great time doing it.

I had a small pro-Kerry Web site up before the 2004 election. After the disappointing loss in November, I decided only two issues really mattered: verifiable/fair voting and media.

"I chose to work on media because I'm a librarian, and I think access to information is *vital* to democracy. In my community, there was a real need for some kind of network to get messages, news, and other communications out to progressives. So I added more local political links and a blog to my site. One link was for Air America Radio (AAR). At that time we could listen to it only on satellite radio or by streaming Internet audio. I started getting more traffic, with people commenting about the things they heard on Air America.

"Then I discovered Meetup (*www.meetup.com*). I set up a fan group, which I called Dallas Air America Radio Meetup Group. I thought if we could get together as fans of AAR, we might get also together as progressives and do something to make a difference. I announced it on my site and spread the word through Daily Kos (Tex_Kos), Democratic Underground, and local lists like Keep Dallas Plastic (a wiki community board at *keepdallas.editme.com*). The first meeting was at my house—15 people came. We now meet once a month, and get 50 to 100 each time.

"Meetup makes the whole process so easy: Once people join a group, all the organizer needs do is set up the events online with a date, time, location. Meetup sends invitations with a Google map link and allows members to RSVP. They can also prepay for events that have a fee or suggested donation amount, using PayPal—I never have to worry about collecting money. Meetup sends out event reminders and even asks for feedback afterwards—so everyone gets a chance to sound off about what they liked (or didn't) about what we did. It's a great tool.

"To talk about news and exchange articles quickly every day, we set up a Yahoo group. There are about 200 members; we say that if you can keep up with our e-mail, you know everything you need to know about what's happening in the news. Our members represent *all* kinds of progressives in the local area; so now we have instantaneous communication among groups that didn't used to be connected in any way. And we have experts on every issue. The more we stay together, the smarter we all get."

When Air America came to a local station in Dallas, Nancy's group volunteered to help with promotion. "I took a page from Howard Dean. His supporters wore Dean T-shirts and became 'Dean Corps' to do community service. So we started volunteering at events like picnics, and film festivals and theatre performances in our Air America T-shirts to advertise our new station and show our true Democrat values.

"Now we've got 300+ people in six counties involved, and other activities have developed, like a film group, and a progressive book group that we also organized using Meetup—it allows members to send title suggestions and vote on what we'll read next.

"All these things are very important because progressives tend to splinter off and get isolated from each other. We tell people, 'You need to join us, because we just have fun.' But really, our job is networking—and getting more people involved. And we do take that very seriously."

GETTING TOGETHER
Tools for doing what Nancy did:
• Check out Dallas Air America's Web site: *www.dallasairamerica.org* Learn about Nancy's group and contact them with questions.
• **Meetup.com:** Great for organizing a gathering. A Meetup Group shares a cause or interest and meets regularly face-to-face. There are thousands of local groups for thousands of interests. For relatively small groups it's secure...and very helpful. (*en.wikipedia.org/wiki/Meetup*)
• **Evite** (*www.evite.com*) is a good way to keep track of who can come to your gathering. And *www.meetingwizard.com* lets you to propose several meeting times and find out the best option for your participants.
• **Communication tools:** YahooGroups and GoogleGroups, for example, offer a simple tool for not-too-complicated projects—e-mail lists (we used to call them listservs) that are free and easy to set up. But first decide whether you want it to be public or private.
• **Heads up!** CivicSpace is an open-source (free) software toolset designed for grassroots groups seeking an efficient way to self-organize through the Web. Used by over 1,000 organizations worldwide, their tools allow users to publish a Web site, manage contacts, send mass e-mails, organize events, create discussion groups, and much more. CivicSpace currently requires savvy technical skills; it will also be available through *civicspacelabs.org* at a nominal fee (about $40 a month).

24. TALK TO A POLITICIAN

According to the Center for Lobbying in the Public Interest, about 20% of the mail Congress gets is postal, 20% is faxed, and 60% is e-mailed.

BACKGROUND. Starting with grade school, we're told constantly that if we want to change things in the U.S., we should write to Congress...or city hall...or the state house. "It's a democracy—your elected representatives listen to you," our teachers always insisted.

Surprisingly enough...they were right. Politicians do want to know what you're thinking—partly because they know that there are plenty of well-funded incumbents who were turned out of office because they lost touch with the voters back home.

But it doesn't matter why they do it. The important thing is that your letters and phone calls *are* effective tools for influencing them. Consider this a reminder: If we want progressive voices to be heard, we have to let elected officials know where we stand.

GETTING THROUGH

• The best way to reach your congressperson is by telephoning their local office (find it in the phone book or online). Local offices don't get as many calls as Capitol Hill, so staffers have more time for you. And they always forward your info to Washington, D.C.

• If you don't want to call, a letter, postcard, or fax is also effective. Again, writing to the local office is best. Letters sent to congressional offices in Washington, D.C., are screened for anthrax; it can take as long as a month and letters are sometimes destroyed in the process.

• E-mails are a last resort; congressional offices are deluged with them and don't read them all. However, e-mail *campaigns* conducted by groups like MoveOn.org can be effective. As Mary Jean Collins of People For the American Way says, "Let's be realistic—getting 100,000 of *anything* has to have an impact."

To contact the Democratic Congressional Campaign Committee: www.dccc.org

TALKING POINTS

• Be courteous. Keep your message short and to the point.

• Focus on a single issue that concerns you; explain how it affects you and the people around you. Talk about what you're for, not what you're against.

• Personal letters are always better than "cookie-cutter" form letters written by special-interest groups. (But you can draw from a form letter to write a personal letter of your own.)

• If you're concerned with a particular bill that's pending in Congress, identify the bill by its title or number if possible.

• If you have a news article or fact sheet that supports your point of view, include that, too.

• When an elected official you've contacted takes your side in an issue or votes your way on a piece of legislation, contact them again and thank them! It's important for elected officials to know that progressive voters are keeping tabs.

MEETING AND GREETING

• The ACLU reminds us: "Members of Congress spend much of their time in their home districts. They often meet with constituents and special-interest groups, or hold community open houses or town halls, or when running for reelection, candidate forums for the public." That's true for state and local politicians too.

• Three good ways to talk to a politician in person: Go to a town hall meeting or other event where they're speaking (ask questions or make a comment); schedule a face-to-face meeting locally; schedule a meeting at their Washington, D.C., office.

RESOURCES

• **People For the American Way** (*www.pfaw.org*) Don't know who to write to? Get names, addresses and phone numbers of your elected representatives here. Go to the Action Center on their website. Click on "Find Elected Officials," type in address or zip code.

• **C-SPAN** (*www.c-span.org/resources*)

• **Peace Action** (*www.peace-action.org/tools/act/howto.html*)

• For local officials, see the Local Government pages in your phone book.

"All that is necessary for the triumph of evil is that good men do nothing." —Edmund Burke

25. JUST SHOW UP

"The world is run by those who show up." —**Ron Nehring,**
Vice-Chairman of the California Republican Party

BACKGROUND. Democracy takes work. It's not enough just to *have* institutions like school boards and planning commissions—someone's got to participate; someone's got to show up. Stephen Gardiner, writing for the *Coalition for Human Dignity,* observes:

> Far away from the scrutiny of a presidential election or high-profile piece of legislation, local institutions—school boards, libraries, hospitals, citizens' commissions, neighborhood associations—are the key battlegrounds in grassroots politics.

Right-wing activists understand this and have used it to their advantage. When they care about an issue, they work to influence it on the local level. They go to town hall meetings and voice their opinions. They attend city council and school board meetings. They let people know exactly where they stand...which has a big impact on the decisions that are made.

Are you willing to do the same?

TO SHOW UP OR NOT TO SHOW UP...

What happens when you don't show? It can affect issues like:

• **Separation of church and state.** In 2005, Louisiana's state government decided to leave curriculum choice to local school boards. The result: Eight boards decided, at public meetings, to adopt a Bible curriculum produced by a private Christian fundamentalist group whose goal is proselytizing to American youth.

• **Civil liberties.** In 2003, 77 people were arrested during a peaceful protest in Sacramento, California, despite their having obtained all necessary permits. Why? A few days earlier, the city council had quietly passed two unconstitutional ordinances—and no one stopped them. The new regulations limited the size of protest signs, specified what materials could be used in their construction, and prohibited possession of items like glass containers, golf balls, and "non-rectangular pieces of wood."

#1 reason registered voters don't vote? "Too busy with work or school on election day."

SIMPLE THINGS YOU CAN DO
Show up!
• You have power at public meetings—all you have to do is stand up and speak. In fact, just being there makes a difference. "Without oversight," one activist says, "things slip by; the government can make important decisions without citizens knowing it. But if there's just one person or reporter there, officials have to be careful about what they're doing." The flip side: By not showing up, you abdicate your power as a citizen.

Go to...
• **School board, city council,** planning commission, or other municipal meetings. You can be sure the Right will be there.

• **Town hall meetings.** These are forums where elected officials or candidates come and speak about community issues. They're often the only place politicians get direct input from community members about their concerns. In 2005, for example, town hall meetings about Social Security were the vehicle that let Congress know America wasn't buying Bush's "reform" plan.

• **Public hearings.** The main purpose of most public hearings "is to obtain public testimony or comment" about an issue—anything from, say, land-use planning to HIV/AIDS education in public schools. Public comments often have a considerable impact on the decisions—and in any case, it's your chance to be heard. These meetings are usually listed in local newspapers.

• **And while you're at it, join a service organization** like Rotary, Kiwanis, Zonta, or Lions. You don't just show up—you have to become a member. But these groups are "incubators" for community leadership and great places to network. Being active in your community means you're one of the gang, not an outsider, which makes your progressive messages and suggestions credible.

RESOURCES
Find schedules for municipal meetings in local newspapers. Or contact your local government or school district. Find their offices in the blue pages of the phone book. You can also find links to local government at: *www.govengine.com/localgov/index.html*

"If you want to make enemies, try to change something." —Woodrow Wilson

"PUBLIC" ENEMIES

*One way or another, these folks are going to undermine
public education if we give them a chance.*

O nly stupid parents would leave their children in the
filthy, immoral, dangerous, public 'education' institutions."

—**J.M. Sutherland, Ph.D,**
The Christian Alert Network

"There are 15,700 school districts in America. When we get an
active Christian parents' committee in all districts, we can take
complete control of all local school boards. This would allow us to
determine all local policy; select good textbooks; good curriculum
programs; superintendents and principals. Our time has come!"

—**Robert Simonds,**
Citizens for Excellence in Education

"I hope I will live to see the day when, as in the early days of our
country, we won't have any public schools. The churches will have
taken them over again and Christians will be running them. What
a happy day that will be!"

—**Rev. Jerry Falwell,** *America Can Be Saved!*

"School vouchers [will] prevent...public school teachers from car-
rying out their liberal social experiment on our children: Teaching
them to hate America, distrust their parents, and believe that big
government is the solution to all of society's ailments."

—**Mark Smith,** *The Official Handbook of the
Vast Right Wing Conspiracy*

"The Christian community has a golden opportunity to train an
army of dedicated teachers who can invade the public school classrooms and use them to influence the nation for Christ."

—**Dr. James Kennedy,** *Coral Ridge Ministries*

Location of the first public high school in America? Boston, in 1820.

26. SUPPORT PUBLIC EDUCATION

"We don't...know what event will trigger the collapse of support for government schools. What we do know is that we are further along than most people think." —Marshall Fritz,
Alliance for the Separation of School and State

BACKGROUND. Public education is a cornerstone of American democracy. The public schools aren't perfect, of course—we all know there are problems that need to be solved. But polls show that most Americans would rather fix our schools than abandon them.

The Radical Right, on the other hand, has been trying to undermine public education for decades. That may come as as surprise to you, but there's really no other way to put it: A well-funded coalition of fundamentalist Christians who believe their children are being poisoned with secular values, and anti-tax crusaders intent on privatizing everything, are doing all they can to push public education to the brink.

They won't stop...which means that people like us, who cherish public schools and everything they stand for, have to fight for them. If not, an essential part of our culture will be lost.

SUPPORTING THE SCHOOLS
Every citizen can make a difference for public schools. For example:
• The Ashland Schools Foundation, a "local educational fund" (LEF) in Ashland, Oregon, raises over $200,000 a year from residents. They provide grants to public schools for choir, drama, tutoring, software, etc.

• Parents for Public Schools in Starkville, Mississippi, has fashioned itself as a "public school promotional organization," recruiting families to enroll their children in public schools. They've played a strategic role in maintaining racial balance in schools through outreach and a successful advertising campaign.

• After volunteering in a local school, Miami lawyer Jamie Rosenberg left his law practice and founded Adopt-A-Classroom

Something to be proud of: In 1900, 6% of U.S. teens graduated high school; in 1996, 85% did.

(*www.adoptaclassroom.com*), a group that matches classes with donors who provide $500 for school supplies—the estimated amount of their own money teachers spend on classes each year.

SIMPLE THINGS YOU CAN DO

Supporting public education is fighting the Right.

Educate Yourself

• Learn about real education reform, such as "evidence-based reform" and "value-added modeling." Start with this *Washington Monthly* article by Thomas Toch (*www.washingtonmonthly.com/features/2005/0510.toch.html*)

• Contact the National Education Association (NEA), the largest education advocacy organization in the U.S., which is under constant attack from the Right. For info: *www.nea.org*

• Read and subscribe to *Rethinking Schools*, print or online (*www.rethinkingschools.org*). Essential reading.

• Read "Defending Public Education" (*www.publiceye.org/ark/education/brochure.html*)

Get Involved

• Attend school board meetings; better yet, run for school board.

• Volunteer; call your local school district to find out how. Talk to teachers to find out what help they need from the community.

• Join or establish a "local education fund" (LEF), an independent nonprofit group that supports public education and is a link between the community and its schools. LEFs are one of the only effective mechanisms for overcoming massive funding cuts and keeping schools healthy. For info, go to Public Education Network (*www.publiceducation.org/lefs.asp*) and California Consortium of Education Foundations (*www.cceflink.org*).

MORE RESOURCES

• **National Coalition for Parent Involvement in Education** (*www.ncpie.org*)

• **Parents for Public Schools** (*www.parents4publicschools.com*) Also has a great page of links.

Take action: (*www.pfaw.org/go/public_education*)
(*www.resultsforamerica.org/education*)

THE WAR ON EDUCATION

"I think it's a lot easier to kill the beast when you get in the cave." —Rep. Tom Tancredo (R-CO), after his appointment to the House education committee

It may be hard to accept the idea that there's really a "war on public education." But there is. And it isn't just a matter of conservatives wanting to tinker with the system, offering a few thoughtful reforms—it's a full-scale assault. As the Commonweal Institute puts it in their report *Responding to the Attack on Public Education*:

> The Right wants to dismantle the entire system of federal and state control over public education and give free rein to commercial and private interests.

One of progressives' weaknesses in this battle is that we believe so strongly in public education, it seems inconceivable that anyone could oppose it. And most Americans agree—so in public, the Right plays down its opposition. But in right-wing publications, you'll hear a different story. Thomas Johnson of the Future of Freedom Foundation is a typically rabid "anti-statist." He says:

> Famous supporters of public education include Hitler, Stalin, Castro, Mao Zedong, Mussolini…. The best possible reform that could ever be effected is eliminating the completely politicized socialist government schools and replacing them with private, profit-making, and charitable education businesses that offer courses of instruction only to willing customers. We need to introduce education to the free market.

But don't assume that only the nuttiest of the Right thinks this way. It's pervasive. As Reed Hundt, head of the FCC under Clinton, wrote in the blog TPM Cafe:

> When I was chairman of the Federal Communications Commission (1993–97), I asked [William] Bennett to visit my office so that I could ask him for help in seeking legislation that would pay for Internet access in all classrooms and libraries in the country…. Since Mr. Bennett had been Secretary of Education [under Ronald Reagan], I asked him to support the bill in the crucial stage when we needed Republican allies. He told me he would not help, because he did not want

public schools to obtain new funding, new capability, new tools for success. He wanted them, he said, to fail so that they could be replaced with vouchers, charter schools, religious schools, and other forms of private education.

Is it difficult to believe that someone who served at such a high level of government—someone America trusted to promote and protect public education—actually despises it? Get used to the idea—people who think like Bennett are now running the whole education department. Thanks to the Bush administration and Republicans in Congress, their views are now institutionalized in America's public schools. The two most egregious examples of this are vouchers and No Child Left Behind.

VOUCHERS, OR "SCHOOL CHOICE"

• Vouchers are a financial credit the government gives parents to send their children to private schools (including religious schools). The money comes out of funds designated for public education.

• The idea was introduced in 1955 by economist Milton Friedman as part of his plan—a blueprint for the right wing ever since—for privatizing all government services. It was then pushed by segregationists to prevent public school integration after the 1954 *Brown v. Board of Education* decision.

• The idea was resurrected by right-wing Christian fundamentalists and "Movement Conservatives" in the 1980s, and supported by an huge right-wing infrastructure that has put hundreds of millions of dollars into marketing, supporting, and legitimizing the concept. On its own, the Bradley Foundation (see page 64) has pumped $355 million into establishing and promoting voucher programs.

• There are now four voucher programs in the U.S. The Right calls them a success, but there's no way to know; like all private schools, "voucher schools" aren't accountable to any government agency. There are no minimum standards, and there's no required assessment testing. Most of the studies that trumpet their success are funded by right-wing foundations.

Resources: Good article to start with:
www.rethinkingschools.org/archive/16_01/Joyc161.shtml
Trace the segregationist roots of "School Choice":
www.rethinkingschools.org/archive/16_01/Lies161.shtml

• Commonweal Institute's excellent report, "Responding to the Attack on Public Education: *www.commonwealinstitute.org/reports/ed/EdRespondReport.html*

• People For the American Way's voucher page (*www.pfaw.org/pfaw/general/default.aspx?oid=9848*) and their report "Voucher Veneer" (*www.pfaw.org/pfaw/general/default.aspx?oid=11371*)

• Read the Milwaukee *Journal Sentinal's* in-depth look at its city's voucher program after 15 years: *www.jsonline.com/news/choice.*

No Child Left Behind (NCLB)

In 2001, the Bush administration passed the No Child Left Behind Act (NCLB), with bipartisan support in Congress. Democrats thought they were compromising to improve public education, but in fact, NCLB appears to have been specifically designed to fail...and to undermine public education in the process.

Consider this: If the idea is to improve schools, why is the act massively underfunded...and why are a majority of states unable to meet even the most minimal of its annual testing standards? In a recent study, for example, it was projected that 93% of Connecticut's schools, 99% of California's, 77% Pennsylvania's, 75% of Massachusetts', 85% of Indiana's, 84% of Wisconsin's, 80% of Ohio's, 85% of Minnesota's, 85% of Illinois', and 100% of Michigan's...*will be labeled failures*. And that's only a partial list. In other words, over a 10-year period, practically every school in America would officially be considered a failure. And what would we have instead? Can anyone say "privatization"?

Resources: Read *Rethinking Schools* articles about NCLB, especially "Why the Right Hates Public Education" by Barbara Miner: *www.rethinkingschools.org/special_reports/bushplan*

• A report on how NCLB is failing in the states, and how they are rebelling: *www.nclbgrassroots.org/landscape.php*

• The NEA's info on NCLB: *www.nea.org/esea*

• An exhaustive list of research and resources at Fair Test *www.fairtest.org/nattest/bushtest.html*

27. GOT CULTURE?

In 1995, the Republican Congress tried to eliminate the National Endowment for the Arts, an agency set up 30 years earlier to provide grants to artists. They failed, but still cut its budget by 40%.

BACKGROUND. What is it about the arts in America that's so threatening to the Radical Right? Is it the way artists inspire new ideas and challenge traditional values? Is it the way artists make it their business—literally—to exercise their right to free speech?

Whatever it is, America needs more of it—and there's an easy way to make sure we get it: Support the arts in your community. Go to a play, see a concert, buy a painting, enjoy a stand-up comedian (especially a political satirist).

As Sue Carney, a performer with the Oregon Shakespeare Festival, says:

> We cannot expect those who do not value free speech to support those who practice it…. If artists are to survive, it is up to us to defend and support them…. An artist shouldn't have to seek funding from fundamentalists. We should take care of our own.

ART ATTACKS
How does the Right try to suppress America's arts and artists?

• **Cutting funding:** Government arts support is rapidly being withdrawn, even locally. Local funding has fallen about 15% since 2002; state funding has fallen almost 40%.

• **Intimidation:** In 2003, the right-wing media went ballistic when the Dixie Chicks criticized George Bush at a concert. The group's CDs were collected and destroyed; radio stations refused to play their music; they even got death threats. They had to install metal detectors at every concert. (But their CD sales actually went up.)

• **Censorship:** In 2005, an artist in Roseville, Michigan, was sentenced to prison for painting a version of Michelangelo's *Creation of Man* on the outside wall of a building. His crime: indecency, for showing Eve with a bare breast.

- **Assault and battery:** Yes, it can even get physical. In 2004, a San Francisco gallery owner was punched and knocked out (her nose was broken) because one painting in a show depicted Abu Ghraib, the Iraqi jail where American soldiers abused prisoners. She closed her gallery because she feared for her children's safety.

SIMPLE THINGS YOU CAN DO

Support Local Arts and Artists

- Don't let the Radical Right's tactics go unanswered. Make an effort to show your support by going to plays, concerts, museums, comedy clubs, galleries, dance performances. It's a most enjoyable way to fight the culture wars. Invite friends to join you—there's strength in numbers.

- Volunteer to help an arts group. You can be pretty sure that any group you choose needs help, but can't afford to pay for it.

- Donate money. Many community arts groups are nonprofits that depend on contributions to survive. Bonus: Every dollar you give is a poke at the Religious Right.

Become an Advocate

There are many ways to make a difference for the arts in America. Check the resources below for ideas and details on how to affect legislation, funding, public support, etc.

RESOURCES

- **Americans for the Arts:** Great advocacy group with events, resources, and suggestions for writing letters to newspapers and politicians. Also includes a directory to help find arts organizations wherever you live. 1-202-371-2830 (*www.artsusa.org*)

- **Assn. of Performing Arts Presenters:** Another excellent Web site. Get educated about the issues that matter to local arts groups. 1-888-820-ARTS or 1-888-820-2787 (*www.artspresenters.org*)

- **Community Arts Network:** "Supports the belief that the arts are an integral part of a healthy culture…and that community-based arts provide significant value both to communities and artists." (*www.communityarts.net*)

- **Arts Over America:** Links to states arts groups. Click on their "Arts-Related sites" for links. (*www.nasaa-arts.org*)

Poll results: 93% of Americans believe the arts "are vital to providing a well-rounded education."

28. TALK BACK TO YOUR TV

In January 2006, Rev. Donald Wildmon, head of the American Family Association, announced—in conjunction with a boycott of a show called The Book of Daniel—*that he was sick of NBC-TV's "anti-Christian bigotry." The show was cancelled.*

BACKGROUND. Television is one of the most powerful forces in our culture. To a large extent, it defines what matters to Americans. It helps shape every decision we make.

The Radical Right has understood this for a long time—which is why they've put so much effort into lobbying TV networks and sponsors. They rail against alleged liberal bias, immorality, religious discrimination—whatever sounds plausible and excites their base. What they really want, of course, is the power to control the content of TV, and publicity for their "culture wars."

And what have progressives done to fight back? Until recently, not much. But that's changing. Internet communities, outraged by right-wing bias on TV, are beginning to organize boycotts and protests. Now your help is needed to keep up the momentum and make sure our voices are the ones the networks listen to.

WHO'S GOT THE POWER?

• In October 2004, the Sinclair Broadcasting Group, a Republican contributor that owns 62 stations in 39 cities, was forced to pull an anti-Kerry "documentary" it had scheduled to run in prime time. The reason? A massive protest by progressive and Democratic groups that resulted in a boycott of local sponsors, a 10% drop in Sinclair's stock, and threats of action by stockholders.

• In January 2006, Katie Couric of the *Today Show* insisted incorrectly in an interview with Howard Dean that convicted lobbyist Jack Abramoff had given money to both Republicans and Democrats. By the next day, progressive Web sites were on the war path. They offered downloadable feeds of the interview, links to correct info about Abramoff's money, and contact information for the

Today Show so people could demand a correction.

• When Chris Matthews, host of MSNBC's *Hardball*, unapologetically compared progressive filmmaker Michael Moore to Osama bin Laden in January 2006, bloggers set up a Web site called *www.openlettertochrismatthews.com* and began a boycott, encouraging sponsors to drop the show.

SIMPLE THINGS YOU CAN DO

Two main areas you can have an impact: Offsetting the Right's complaints (see p. 118), and protesting when progressive voices aren't heard. Speak up. Unless networks, sponsors, and the FCC know you're out there and ready to fight, they'll take the path of least resistance and hand TV over to the Radical Right.

• **Contact the networks and their local affiliates.** You can call, fax, e-mail, or send letters directly to the stations. Make sure to reference the show details, your support or criticism of the program, and whether you'll keep watching it. Let them know that you'll be contacting their advertisers as well.

• **Write or call advertisers.** Explain how their program endorsements will affect your buying decisions.

• **Communicate with the Federal Communications Commission** (FCC). Right-wing groups make a big deal about filing complaints with the FCC, but it's mostly spin. The FCC has no power to change or affect any broadcast content (though they can fine broadcasters for indecency). But it still makes sense to contact them and register support for programming you know is under assault from the Right: *www.fcc.gov/cgb/ecfs*

• **Spread the word.** E-mail friends and community groups, contact print media, or post a comment on a blog. Radio and TV call-in shows are a way to convey your message to a larger, or specifically targeted, audience. For info on how to "talk back" on call-in shows, check out *www.callingallwingnuts.com*

RESOURCE

Progressive Democrats of America Their media guide supplies local and national contact info. (*capwiz.com/pdamerica/dbq/media*)

GIVE 'EM A WEDGIE

"As we all know, a 'wedge issue' is a campaign topic that works well for Republicans and poorly for Democrats."
—**Jonah Goldberg, The National Review**

USING THE WEDGE

One of the Right's most effective political strategies has been the use of "wedge issues."
A wedge issue, according to columnist William Safire, is "a subject that splits a coalition or constituency."

"For example," says linguist George Lakoff, "conservatives are using the 'partial-birth abortion' initiative to drive a wedge between progressives, splitting off the support of Catholics—who traditionally oppose abortion but who also tend to favor progressive policies for the poor—from other progressives who generally support women's reproductive freedom."

Why should partial-birth abortion (a political term, not a medical one, by the way) attract so much fuss? After all, the procedure is done only rarely, often to save the woman's life. Because wedge issues, Lakoff explains, are symbols that "stand in for the whole of a moral system."

THE MORAL OF THE STORY

Bernie Horn of the Center for Policy Alternatives takes the idea a step further: "One reason wedge issues are so effective is that in a political campaign, all issues are symbolic. They express values rather than policy. So the trick to having a campaign strategy is finding issues where a wide majority sides with you, and where your opponent is forced to take the other side.

"Look at school prayer, for example. Sure, it's unconstitutional, but the majority of Americans support it. So if the Right can turn it into the focus of a campaign, and we oppose it—which, as a matter of principle, we have to—it can define an election, making progressives seem anti-religious or immoral." The election is then about morality—as opposed to, say, how to fix the economy or improve education.

Great article: "The Progressive Wedge"...

Horn continues; "The goal isn't to come up with a clever retort to the Right's messaging—it's to push back with our own wedge issues—change the subject to something on which we side with the majority. Look at it this way—the undecided, persuadable voters will go with either us or the other side, depending what they think the election is about. If it's 1992, and the election is about 'the economy, stupid,' they have to vote for Clinton. If it's 2004, and the election is about the War on Terror, they're Bush supporters.

"The challenge in a campaign is not to change people's minds—it's to explain to them why they were for you all along. It's about walking them through the right door."

THE CHALLENGE

Progressives have to learn to use wedge issues effectively—to frame our issues so they highlight our strengths and expose the hidden goals of our opponents. "That means stepping back and separating the conventional wisdom and insider thinking from what people really want," Horn explains. "It can be difficult—people on the inside of a debate are often unaware that something's a wedge issue." But we've got plenty to work with. Lakoff suggests, for example:

> Clean air and clean water can be made into an effective wedge issue, since this is something that many conservatives also value deeply. Progressives could campaign for poison-free communities by focusing on how mercury poisons the air we breathe, and the water we drink and fish in. As a wedge issue, it would split off conservatives who care about their own health and their children's health from those who oppose government regulations generally—the issue divides the traditional conservative coalition. Successfully framing the issue as one in which regulation promotes health would put opponents on the defensive, putting them in the untenable and awkward position of opposing health if they opposed regulation.

What are some other potential wedges? Horn suggests:
• **Energy Efficiency:** A chance to talk about national security, high prices, our families, and the environment.
• **Privacy and Identity Theft:** Under the Bush administration, everyone's privacy is at risk. Privacy and identity theft legislation allows candidates to champion individual privacy and lead the fight on crime.
• **Prescription Drugs:** Bush's Medicare plan is a political disaster. Voters are likely to welcome alternative policies.

...by Bernie Horn (www.tompaine.com/article/2006/01/20/the_progressive_wedge.php)

29. INVESTMENT STRATEGY

"A leader is a dealer in hope."
—*Napoleon Bonaparte*

BACKGROUND: Have you ever heard of the Leadership Institute in Arlington, Virginia? Most people haven't. But for 27 years it's played a key role in politics, preparing literally tens of thousands of right-wingers to move into positions of power in America.

Does that sound incredible? In fact, conservatives spend almost $45 million a year on their campus organizations and "leadership" training institutes. Every year they teach thousands of promising young conservatives to advance the right-wing agenda, offering courses with names like "How to Frame the Environment Issue" and "How to Stop Liberals in Their Tracks." Plus, they have internships, fellowships, and jobs waiting for graduates.

The impact? Well, Karl Rove was trained when he was in his early 20s. So were Supreme Court Justice Samuel Alito, Ralph Reed, Grover Norquist, Ann Coulter—even Jack Abramoff. The list also includes dozens of members of Congress, more than 200 state legislators, several former governors, judges, and many media personalities. You get the idea.

Can progressives compete? The Right has a big head start, but we're ready to play. We've finally got our own leadership institutes and training courses, and they're already working with the next generation of progressive leaders. But they could use a hand.

GETTING STARTED
• Rockwood Leadership has trained over 1,400 individuals from 800 progressive organizations.
• Since 2003, their first year in existence, the Center for Progressive Leadership has trained almost 1,000 political leaders
• In 2005, Wellstone Action trained more than 2,800 activists and candidates, raising their total since 2003 (their first year) to

more than 9,000. In 2005, 15 Camp Wellstone graduates were elected to office—making a total of 35 elected candidates in two years.

• Young People For the American Way has made long-term investment in 1,300 young, emerging program leaders and activists from more than 60 campuses in 18 states.

SIMPLE THINGS YOU CAN DO

• **Nominate a leader.** Let progressive training organizations know who's out there. If you know a young person who has the passion, intelligence, and drive to become an effective leader, nominate them to receive training. Contact: *www.youngpeoplefor.org/nominate*

• **Be a sponsor.** Make a donation to help get someone to the next level. Any amount makes a difference. The Right spends a literal fortune on this; we have to put money into it, too. Contact: *www.progressleaders.org/donate/index.htm*, *www.youngpeoplefor.org /support*, or *www.rockwoodleadership.org/donation.html*

• **Mentor someone.** Many young people rely on volunteers like you to acquire leadership skills. If you know a student who seems promising, just start working with them. Lend whatever expertise and moral support you can.

RESOURCES

These groups are the ground floor of the movement to train progressives to become America's leaders of tomorrow:

• **Rockwood Leadership** (*www.rockwoodleadership.org*). Leadership and collaboration training for organizations and individuals.

• **Young People For the American Way** (YPFAW). "Empowers and engages the next generation of progressive leaders, who will protect and advance our nation's core values." (*www.youngpeoplefor.org*)

• **Wellstone Action Leadership Trainings.** Especially focused on training activists. Weekend trainings offer practical tools to "take back to your community so you can become the leaders we deserve." (*www.wellstone.org*) 1-615-645-3939

• **Center for Progressive Leadership.** "Provides an emerging leader with the tools, resources, and knowledge to be successful." (*www.progressleaders.org*)

• **Western Institute for Organizing and Leadership Development** (WILD). (*www.westernstatescenter.org*)

30. STAND UP FOR SCIENCE

In 2005, there were active anti-evolution movements in 40 states.

BACKGROUND. In the early 1600s, Galileo insisted the earth circled the sun. The Catholic Church disagreed, declaring that the Bible proved the sun revolved around the earth. And just to drive home their point, they imprisoned Galileo for life.

Today the Christian Right is playing the part of the medieval Church, insisting once again that science should be subordinate to religious doctrine.

They're trying to undermine science on many fronts, but their main battleground is evolution.

UNDERMINING SCIENCE

• The Christian Right intentionally misrepresents evolution. For example, they insist it's "atheistic." Actually, the theory deals only with natural processes and doesn't address the existence of God *at all*. In fact, in a recent poll, 62% of natural scientists—and 59% of all biologists—said they believe in God.

• Anti-evolutionists want science classes to teach intelligent design (ID), the theory that life's complexity requires an intelligent force behind it. But science is based on testing hypotheses with experiments. ID *cannot be tested*—so it's not science, it's philosophy.

• Attacking evolution is just a start. Who knows what's next? Already, says the *New York Times*, "scriptural literalists are moving beyond evolution, to challenge the teaching of geology and physics on issues like the age of the earth and the origin of the universe."

• We're already behind other countries in science education: In the 2003 PISA survey of science literacy, American schoolkids came in 22nd out of 41 industrialized nations. At a time when America is trying to stay competitive internationally, the Christian Right wants to push us even further behind.

More info on evolution: National Association of Biology Teachers (www.nabt.org/sub/evolution)

SIMPLE THINGS YOU CAN DO

Support Science Education in School. Talk to teachers—find out how to help. Polls say 31% of public school teachers feel pressure to downplay evolution. Let them know you're on *their* side.

• *Support science fairs.* They're a great experience for kids and a public statement that your community supports science.

• *Keep an eye on school boards and school board elections.* School boards determine local policy. If a hearing is held, speak up. The National Center for Science Education (see below) has "12 Tips for Testifying at School Board Meetings" in their Resource section.

• *Challenge school board candidates on evolution.* Anti-evolutionists sometimes run as "stealth" candidates; their views aren't clear until after they're elected.

• *Encourage a scientist to run for your local school board.*

Make Evolution a Local and State Campaign Issue.

• *Get politicians to address the issue during the election campaign.* Don't waste your time trying to convince creationists about evolution. Just get out and vote.

• *Protect statewide science-curriculum standards.* Demand that candidates for the state board of education clearly define their positions on evolution. Find out from your school board who's in charge of setting the standards; monitor their actions.

• *Support science museums.* They're a key source of public science education. Become a member, volunteer, encourage others to go.

• *Learn about evolution.* Be honest—how much do you really know? Check out the resources below, so you can stand your ground in discussions about ID, creationism, and evolution.

RESOURCES

National Center for Science Education: (*www.ncseweb.org*) The only national group dedicated to the issue—a clearinghouse for info.

National Science Teachers Association: (*www.nsta.org*) Has support for pro-evolution teachers and parents.

Understanding Evolution: (*evolution.berkeley.edu*) A Web site about evolution, from the University of California at Berkeley.

Evolutionblog: (*evolutionblog.blogspot.com*)

Recommended film: *Inherit the Wind* (1960), starring Spencer Tracy. Evolution on trial.

THE WAR ON SCIENCE

"The Bush administration has declared war on science. In the Orwellian world of 21st century America, two plus two no longer equals four where public policy is concerned, and science is no exception. When a right-wing theory is contradicted by an inconvenient scientific fact, the science is not refuted; it is simply discarded or ignored." —**Howard Dean**

N O PLAN B
The emergency contraception pill called "Plan B" has been available with a prescription since 1999. In 2003, by a vote of 24 to 3, an FDA advisory panel of scientists recommended that the agency approve the pill for over-the-counter sales.

In 50 years, the FDA had rejected the opinion of an advisory council only once. And in this case, the vote was so lop-sided that it was merely a formality for the acting director of the FDA's Center for Drug Evaluation and Research to approve it. Except that he didn't. He overturned the recommendations of his own staff and declared Plan B, "not approvable" for nonprescription status.

In 2006, it finally came to light that David Hager, a right-wing Christian on the panel who opposed approval, had been asked by the FDA to write a "minority opinion" about the issue. This report was apparently used to justify the decision. "Once again," Hager declared, "what Satan meant for evil, God turned into good."

RESEARCH DEFICIT

Experts say that stem cell research provides us with some of the most promising opportunities to cure disease in the history of medicine. "Given the promise of stem cell research for treating and perhaps curing a variety of debilitating diseases," says the National Academy of Sciences, "[we feel] strongly that research not be limited, but include work on both human adult and embryonic stem cells."

But the Religious Right opposes embryonic stem cell research. So in 2001, President Bush banned federal funding for new stem cell research. However, in an attempt to appear supportive of scientific research, he endorsed using the "more than 60 genetically diverse stem cell lines" that already existed, claiming they "could lead to breakthrough therapies and cures."

Save the Whales? In 2002, Bush weakened rules protecting them...at oil and gas lobbyists' requests.

The problem: His compromise was science fiction, not fact. "Bush made his claim, which startled experts, on the basis of inadequately vetted scientific information," Chris Mooney wrote in *American Progress* in 2004. "Consider the NIH's disclosure…that only 23 lines might ever be available under Bush's policy. This was, arguably, the biotech equivalent of failing to find Saddam's WMD." The stark fact is that Radical Right politics has trumped science…again.

A DIFFERENT VIEW

Scientists say that the Grand Canyon was created between 2 and 5 million years ago, by the combined action of the Colorado River cutting a channel down into the rock and surrounding plateaus being lifted up.

That' the official story. Or at least it was until 2003, when the book store at Grand Canyon National Park began selling *The Grand Canyon: A Different View*, which gives the *creationist* account of the origins of the canyon.

According to Jeffrey St. Clair, of *Counterpunch*, the book is by Tom Vail, a river guide, who offers "Christian float trips" through the canyon. "For years…I told people how the Grand Canyon was formed over the evolutionary time scale of millions of years," Vail writes in the book. "Then I met the Lord. Now, I have 'a different view' of the Canyon, which…can't possibly be more than about a few thousand years old." The book suggests that the canyon was created by Noah's flood. "One thing is sure," it says: "the Colorado River did not do it."

Park rangers wanted to publish a rebuttal of the book so the staff could answer the creationist zealots who often confront them. The Bush administration refused to give them permission.

INSIDE OUT

In testimony to the U.S. Senate in 2001, Bush's Interior Secretary Gale Norton claimed that caribou would not be affected by drilling for oil in the Arctic Refuge, because they calve outside the area targeted for drilling. It was a lie. "Later," writes Robert F. Kennedy, Jr. "she explained that she somehow substituted 'outside' for 'inside.' She also substituted findings from a study financed by an oil company for the ones that the Fish and Wildlife Service had prepared for her."

"The road to tyranny begins with the destruction of the truth." —Bill Clinton

31. BALANCING ACT

"The idea is to divert the attacks of our opponent in such a way as to turn his own force against him." —**The Handbook of Tai Chi**

BACKGROUND. Throughout this book we've suggested ways to join forces with progressive organizations. Now, just for fun, let's turn the process on its head; instead of working *with* a group, let's work *against* one.

OUR INSPIRATION
• In January 2006, the right-wing American Family Association (AFA) began a campaign to boycott *The Book of Daniel*, a TV show that included Jesus as a character. They encouraged AFA members to lobby NBC to cancel the program...but they inspired at least one viewer to do the opposite.

• Here's what she posted on the NBC bulletin board: "I am a Christian and I really enjoyed the program. The reason I watched? I received a forwarded e-mail from...[the] American Family Association telling me to petition my local affiliate to get them *not* to air it.... AFA prides themselves on sending their subscribers 'bulletins' to further their political agenda, but I think the AFA should be given a dose of their own medicine."

• That gave us an idea: We went directly to the media outlets and sponsors that AFA had threatened and expressed our *support* for the show. And (this is the fun part) AFA helped us do it.

• The key: Like most right-wing organizations, they have an excellent Web site with names, phone numbers, and addresses of politicians, media, and corporate sponsors—as well as form letters to adapt and send, expressing our own (opposite) opinions.

SIMPLE THINGS YOU CAN DO
Create an e-mail tree to use the Right's Web sites against them:
• Get together with five friends. Each of you "adopt" one organization (See Resources). Set up a free e-mail account at *hotmail.com* or *yahoo.com* using an "alias" (you have to use a real street address, if they ask). This doesn't just keep you anonymous—it lets you see if

Activist tip: Don't assume someone else is doing it.

your name and e-mail are being shared or sold.

• Go to the group's Web site; sign up for their daily e-mail alerts and newsletters. Note: If you use their letter-writing forms, the site will install "cookies" on your hard drive to check if street addresses are real, and they may keep your information on file. So decide in advance how much of your real info you want to give.

• When you get an e-mail alert that calls for a noxious right-wing action, forward it to your friends. Each of you should make the phone call, send the complaint, or take action as requested—but express a *progressive* view. If the right-wingers are advocating an FCC complaint against your favorite risqué comedian, send your endorsement instead. If they want a business to stop donating to Planned Parenthood, write and tell them PP has your total support.

• Remember: Keep this manageable—don't get so many newsletters that you overdose on right-wing propaganda. There's a high burnout potential.

• Expand the effort: If your five friends tell five other friends, and they all start "anti-e-mail" trees too, you'll be generating thousands of progressive e-mails to offset the Right's attacks.

RESOURCES

Here are 10 of the more active right-wing groups:

• **The Free Congress Foundation** (*www.freecongress.org*)

• **Family Research Council** (*www.frc.org*)

• **American Family Association** (*www.afa.net*)

• **Alliance Defense Fund** (*www.alliancedefensefund.org*)

• **Townhall.com's Action** (*www.townhall.com/action*)

• **Christian Coalition** (*www.christian-coalition.org*)

• **Eagle Forum** (*www.eagleforum.org/misc/subscribe.html*)

• **American Conservative Union** (*www.conservative.org*)

• **Concerned Women for America** (*www.cwfa.org/subscribe.asp*)

• **Life Decisions International** (*www.fightpp.org*)

32. VOLUNTEER FOR A CAMPAIGN

About 63% of voting Americans are volunteers...surprisingly,
only 8% of them volunteer on political campaigns.

BACKGROUND. If you volunteer for political campaigns, you already understand how important this is. If you haven't yet, we urge you to give it a try. There aren't many things you can do (short of running for office yourself) that have more direct impact on a campaign. Your work, presence, and day-to-day support are all invaluable. As one organizer puts it:

> No campaign treasury can afford to pay workers to do the jobs that volunteers do for free. Even if a candidate or organization could afford to pay a salary to every person who participates in a campaign, he or she would be foolish to do so. Volunteers bring to a campaign a dedication and a willingness to work that is indispensable.

THE VOLUNTEER LIFE

• Unlike most other types of volunteering, political campaigns have a defined time frame, and end on a specific date. As a result, the volunteer experience is generally more intense.

• While there are plenty of interesting things to do in a campaign (see Become a Precinct Captain, p. 171), a lot of political volunteering involves "grunt work" like stuffing envelopes and making phone calls. However, if you believe in the overall goal—which is getting progressive candidates elected—then that's all the inspiration you should need.

• You'll get a lot from just being involved. You'll meet other people who believe as strongly as you do...and fighting the Right is as much about local coalition-building as it is about electoral politics. The people you interact with on a campaign will help shape your overall outlook...and you'll help shape theirs.

SIMPLE THINGS YOU CAN DO

Here's an eight-point "to-do list" for potential volunteers:

1. Be prepared. Before you volunteer, think about what you want

Poll results: About 15% of the voting population say they...

your role to be, and how much time you have to give.

If you plan to volunteer on a regular basis, you should be willing to do whatever's needed—from telephoning voters and distributing campaign literature, to walking the district with the candidate or other volunteers.

2. Contact the campaign. You can get the phone number from your county Democratic National Committee headquarters.

3. Speak up. As Catherine Shaw, author of *The Campaign Manager*, points out, it's the campaign's responsibility to put each volunteer in the right place, so they're having a good time. But a volunteer should also know what they like to do. Are you good at data entry but not good on phones? The more you know your strengths and weaknesses, the more help you are to a campaign.

4. Use your best skills. If you have a special talent—e.g., writing press releases or organizing candidate receptions, or if you speak a second language—let the volunteer coordinator know. Blogging is also becoming an important component of campaigns. If you have that or other computer skills, make sure the campaign knows it. For an article on campaign blogging, Google "The Future of Blogs and Campaigns," by Matt Stoller.

5. Anticipate problems. Campaign offices are harried places, and even the most well-intentioned staff members can be overextended. Act on your own behalf—don't be argumentative, but be assertive. This is very important—many causes and campaigns have been torpedoed by the desertion of frustrated volunteers.

6. Volunteer as early in the campaign as possible. People who show an early interest in a campaign are more trusted and are given greater responsibility. (But of course, campaigns always need people right up until the last minute.)

7. Keep your promises. Be consistent. Too many volunteers don't arrive when they say they will, or finish what they start.

8. Think strategically. Make your participation count for even more—inspire others to join you. Volunteer with a friend, a spouse, a parent, or a child. Share your experiences—post comments at a political blog. Write an op-ed for the local newspaper. (See p. 77 for tips.)

...would volunteer for a political campaign—if asked.

OLD PROBLEMS, NEW SOLUTIONS

This piece was contributed by Jefferson Smith, the innovative founder of the Bus Project (see p.177) as a "nonpartisan interlude." He says: "We like to say the Bus Project 'Drives Leaders, Drives Votes, and Drives Ideas.' It's a political incubator—part voter mobilizer and part political school. Everything below is something we've actually tried (successfully), and any of these ideas could be replicated with a smart team of committed and cool people."

OLD PROBLEM: Getting Out The Vote. Studies show that knocking on doors and talking to voters boosts turnout, but how do you get enough folks to do the knockin' and talkin'?

NEW SOLUTION: Trick-or-Vote™! What's the one day you expect people to knock on your door? Halloween...which occurs just days before every November election. In 2004, we gathered friendly, costumed volunteers who knocked on doors to remind people to vote, and we all then returned for a big Halloween bash that night. Nearly 800 volunteers showed in Portland alone—the biggest single canvass we'd ever seen (hundreds of canvassers had never done a political thing before)—and the effort was mirrored in other cities. You might be too old to trick-or-treat, but you're never too old to Trick-or-Vote.

OLD PROBLEM: Modern debates are boring. Few people actually see candidates live and in person. And too many candidate forums are canned-chat snoozefests that attract few people, get little attention, and produce limited follow-up.

NEW SOLUTION: Candidates Gone Wild® Debates: In 2004, working with a local alternative weekly newspaper and a local civic club, we organized "Candidates Gone Wild." The event charged $3, served beer, invited the mayoral and city council candidates of whatever party, and put them through a fun-filled, game-show format of substance and silliness. The event humanized the candidates, took them out of their scripted comfort zone, and exposed them to a different sent of constituents. Nearly 2,000 people attended the two debates, local TV showed up, and many guests became active volunteers. We consider it a gateway drug to the political process.

40% of young people aged 16–25 volunteer for something over the course of a year...

OLD PROBLEM: Informing Busy (or Lazybones) Voters. Many voters don't carefully read the long voters pamphlets about candidates and ballot issues—particularly on local matters. This lack of info gives even more power to big-money outfits who can buy TV ads and expensive direct-mail operations.

NEW SOLUTION: The "2-Minute Voter Guide"®. An average person can read one regular page in just under two minutes. A one-page voter guide can fit key facts about important issues and candidates, and it can be printed on a home printer or copier for pennies per page. What's more, studies confirm that a plain-white "just-the-facts" voter guide can be even more convincing than a spendy, glossy mailer. The "2-Minute Voter Guide" can be stacked in doctor's offices, handed out at doorsteps, included in letters, sent out on the Web, or just kept in the toilet area (where many people spend more than two minutes).

OLD PROBLEM: Making Politics Cool. Any effort trying to engage young people in the political process is competing not merely with some opposing viewpoint, but also with MTV, Xbox, and *US Magazine*.

NEW SOLUTION: Hip-Hop Voter Drive. We mix in music and other fun elements as a reward after our political work—spoonfuls of sugar to help the medicine go down. In 2004, in partnership with a local hip-hop radio station, we organized a mass canvass, voter drive, and hip-hop concert. A concert isn't enough—people might show up for a concert but do nothing else—but having a party or concert as a reward for some good work is a great motivator and friend-raiser. And it also opens up the process to new groups of voters and potential leaders.

OLD PROBLEM: Getting a Group "On Message." It's sometimes hard to keep track of the stuff we're all working for. Different groups fight for different issues, and different people use the word "progressive" differently.

NEW SOLUTION: Remember the "Six E's."™ We focus on a short list of issues—what we call our "Six E's"—Education, Environment, Economy, Equal Rights, Election Reform, and 'Ealth Care (with no "H"). They provide a handy short list; if you can remember the six E's, you're rarely caught flat-tongued.

...but only 2–3% will volunteer for a political candidate or political cause.

33. JOIN THE PARTY

"Thomas Jefferson founded the Democratic Party in 1792 as a congressional caucus to fight for the Bill of Rights." —**www.democrats.org**

BACKGROUND. Even if you've always voted for Democrats, you might be frustrated with the Democratic Party these days. You might be thinking: Why don't more Democrats step up and challenge the radicals who are taking over our country? Why don't the Democrats fight for traditional liberal values? Where is the thundering voice we want to hear condemning the Republicans' corruption and cronyism? Good questions. But the answer is not "I give up." The Democratic Party is a vital weapon in the fight against the Radical Right. If the party needs to change, then we should be the ones to change it.

LEARNING FROM THE RIGHT

• You have more political power than you think. American political parties are actually grassroots organizations, shaped by local volunteers.

• The best proof: the Religious Right. When the Christian Coalition and its allies failed to dictate national policies in the 1980s, they switched their focus to local politics. "[We] got it backwards," explains Ralph Reed, the Coalition's former executive director. "We tried to change Washington, D.C., when we should have been focusing on the states."

• Their new strategy: Use dedicated volunteers to take over local Republican parties, one at a time, then leverage that into control of state parties...and national policy.

• It worked...because in local politics, the people who do the work are the ones who wield the power. "If moderates complain," Reed said about the takeover, "they have to keep in mind that we're the ones licking the envelopes and burning shoe leather."

• By 1996, over 1/4 of the delegates to the national Republican Convention were connected to the Christian Right. They now control much of the national Republican Party.

• Today, progressives have the same opportunity. The Democratic

In 2000, the Christian Coalition reportedly distributed more than 70 *million* voters' guides.

Party is in the throes of an identity crisis. We can help direct it to promote progressive ideals and aggressively take on the Right...or just watch while others decide its direction.

SIMPLE THINGS YOU CAN DO

Register to vote as a Democrat. That's all it takes to join the Democratic Party.

Go to a meeting. Call your local Democrats to find out where they meet. Check the yellow pages under "Political Organizations" for contact info, or find it at *democrats.com.*

Participate. If you disagree about something, say so. If the group's run poorly, get some friends to join...and change it. "Leaders show up," says a Democratic activist. "They're the ones who attend the meetings, ask the stupid questions, follow through, and deliver."

Get involved. It's a volunteer organization—they need help with nearly everything. Your involvement can be limited to stuffing envelopes and manning phone banks, or you can become one of the people who set policy. Talk to the people in charge and find out their procedures for electing local officers.

Become a precinct captain: See p. 171 for details—it's easy.

RESOURCES

- *www.democrats.org* Official Web site of the Democrats
- *www.yda.org* Young Democrats of America
- *www.collegedems.com* College Democrats of America
- *www.democracyforamerica.com* Democracy For America; a group inspired by Howard Dean.
- *www.grassrootsdemocrats.com* Dedicated to strengthening state Democratic Parties.
- *www.pdamerica.org* Progressive grassroots activists who work with Democrats .
- *www.registerfivedemocrats.com/links.htm* Has links to all the local and state Democratic Party Web sites.

"Voting is the life-blood of our democracy." —Lyndon B. Johnson

"WE MUST HAVE A CHRISTIAN NATION"

The Christian Right repudiates the whole idea of separation of church and state. In fact, according to Jerry Falwell, the idea was "invented by the devil to keep Christians from running their own country."

This is our land. This is our world. This is our heritage, and with God's help, we shall reclaim this nation for Jesus Christ. And no power on earth can stop us."
> —Dr. James Kennedy, *Coral Ridge Ministries*

"After the Christian majority takes control, pluralism will be seen as immoral and evil and the state will not permit anybody the right to practice evil."
> —Gary Potter, *Catholics for Christian Political Action*

"Politicians who do not use the Bible to guide their public and private lives do not belong in office."
> —Louis Sheldon, *The Family Research Council*

"The Constitution of the United States is a marvelous document for self-government by Christian people. But the minute you turn the document into the hands of non-Christian people and atheistic people, they can use it to destroy the very foundation of our society."
> —Rev. Pat Robertson, *The 700 Club*

"Many people believe [in the separation of church and state]. The only problem is it's really a deception from Satan."
> —Televangelist Joyce Meyer, *addressing The Christian Coalition*

"Our goal must be simple: We must have a Christian Nation built on God's law, on the Ten Commandments. No apologies."
> —Randall Terry, *founder of Operation Rescue*

Want to see someone fight the Right? Watch Keith Olbermann on MSNBC.

FOR THE

COMMITTED

"HERE'S WHAT *I* DO…"

*More testimonials from the hundreds of grassroots
activists who sent us their ideas for this book.*

I HAVE TAKEN TO INVESTIGATING some of the ridiculous e-mails I receive that are created just to inflame and rally the Radical Right. For example, yesterday I had one with a picture of Marine troops gathered with their heads bowed in prayer, stating that the ACLU was trying to stop them from praying because they were government employees on government land. When I get an e-mail like that, I go to a Web site called *TruthorFiction.com*, which researches e-mails and gives you the real story about them. Then I hit 'reply all' and send the truthful page to everyone who's forwarded the message. I also forward the whole thing to my e-mail list to show others the ways we're being propagandized."
—**Sherryanne Snipes, Massachusetts**

"I TALK TO MY KIDS ABOUT MY BELIEFS. For example, I have avoided Wal-Mart for years. My seven-year-old son often heard me say 'Wal-Mart is destroying our society.' I'm sure it sounded like a radical tirade from an angry mother, rather than a logical response to a real problem. Recently he asked me 'Why?' I took a step back and explained my beliefs, (they treat their employees inadequately, don't provide adequate health coverage, purchase products from companies that treat their employees even worse, etc.). Even at seven he now understands that we can make a difference, and convey a message, by the way we conduct our daily lives."
—**Sunny Spicer, Oregon**

"START AN EDITORIAL WRITERS' GROUP. I pulled a group together locally and we're regularly in several local papers. We call ourselves the Progressive Writers Block (*www.progressivewritersbloc.com*). We circulate and critique each other's articles then send them in for publication and put them on our Web site. We often add links to document our facts or provide additional background in the online versions. This idea is applicable whether you want to write about the environment or other issues. They all run together in the end."
—**David Chandler, California**

34. BECOME AN EXPERT

"Discussion is an exchange of knowledge; an argument an exchange of ignorance." —**Robert Quillen, American humorist**

BACKGROUND. Have you ever found yourself butting heads with someone who's mindlessly spouting right-wing talking points? There's nothing more frustrating. You know the person is full of hot air, but you can't seem to prove it.

This probably isn't what you want to hear, but the problem may be that you don't know what you're talking about. Think about it—have you really taken the time to understand the issues you're discussing? Have you done any research at all?

We've all got opinions...but that doesn't make us experts. The good news: You can learn about practically any subject you choose. The Internet puts a research library at your fingertips; anyone who's willing to do a little work can get a good grip on an issue in a week. Then, when you speak up as a progressive, you'll be self-confident and knowledgeable. And you can finally let the hot air out of that windbag's arguments.

HOW TO RESEARCH A "HOT-BUTTON" ISSUE
Pick one issue at a time, and be open-minded enough to follow the actual research; don't just try to confirm what you think you already know. Here's a general idea of how you do it:

• Let's use "tort reform"—a Republican term for limiting civil lawsuit damages—as an example. First, you'll want to get a basic overview of the subject, including common terminology, so you can understand what people are talking about.

• Do a quick Internet search on the term *tort reform*. The first group listed on our Google search is the American Tort Reform Association; we can instantly tell it's right-wing (giveaway: they use the term "lawsuit abuse"). Next on the list: something from an outfit called Newsbatch, which presents both sides of the issue; we start there. The first progressive entry is eighth on the list, a *Nation* article called "Guess Who's Behind Tort Reform?" Reading selectively, we get an idea of the basic issues.

• Read with an open mind so you can really understand the Right's arguments. It's counterproductive to get angry. There's usually at least a kernel of truth in their position—try to find it, then see how their position develops from there.

• Now go a little deeper. The secret behind Internet research is selecting the right combinations of words. For example, combining "tort reform," "medical malpractice," and "trial lawyers" turns up arguments from each side. Add the term "frivolous" to "medical malpractice" and the slant is more right-wing; add "consumer protection" to "trial lawyers" and you get more from the left. You can also try adding "Radical Right" or "leftist" to your search terms.

• If you run into a dead end, start again and ask the question (or state the issue) in a different way. A few things to try: Combine "trial lawyers" and "Democrats"; "tort reform" and "right-wing commentary"; "Karl Rove" and "tort reform." See what comes up.

• Reading these articles may eventually start to feel confusing or overwhelming. Don't worry—it's all part of the process. Our advice: When you've read enough to feel familiar with the topic, focus primarily on progressive writers who know the subject and have put together an intelligent critique of the Right's position. But stay critical. You're trying to establish yourself as an expert, not just buying someone else's line.

• What will you find out? Well, in the case of tort reform, you might find the insurance industry is behind a lot of the lobbying for these changes in law…that the issue is particularly appealing to Republicans because trial lawyers are major Democratic contributors…that despite "frivolous" lawsuits, the number of doctors is rising, not falling; and that malpractice lawsuits actually add to health care costs by only about 1%. You may also find that tort reform isn't just about medical malpractice lawsuits; it's about *all* civil lawsuits—a much bigger issue that benefits large corporations. But that's just a start. The rest is up to you. There's a lot of fun in debunking the Right's talking points, once you dig in.

• When you become an expert on an issue, you become a resource. Not only will you be able to fight right-wing propaganda, you'll be able to inform other Americans who are hungry for accurate information about issues that affect their lives. And that makes it especially worthwhile.

Lawsuit abuse? George W. Bush sued Enterprise Rent-A-Car for $2,500 in 1999.

GOLDWATER VS. THE RELIGIOUS RIGHT

Here's an unexpected ally: Barry Goldwater, the father of the modern conservative movement, wasn't too fond of the anti-democratic Radical Right. Here's what he said about them.

I am a conservative Republican, but I believe in democracy and the separation of church and state. The conservative movement is founded on the simple tenet that people have the right to live life as they please as long as they don't hurt anyone else in the process."

"I don't have any respect for the Religious Right. There is no place in this country for practicing religion in politics. That goes for Falwell, Robertson, and all the rest of these political preachers. They are a detriment to the country."

"A lot of so-called conservatives don't know what the word means. They think I've turned liberal because I believe a woman has a right to an abortion. That's a decision that's up to the pregnant woman, not up to the Pope or some do-gooders or the Religious Right."

"By maintaining the separation of church and state the United States has avoided the intolerance which has so divided the rest of the world with religious wars.... Can any of us refute the wisdom of Madison and the other framers? Can anyone look at the carnage in Iran, the bloodshed in Northern Ireland, or the bombs bursting in Lebanon and yet question the dangers of injecting religious issues into the affairs of state?"

"The religious issues of these groups have little or nothing to do with conservative or liberal politics. The uncompromising position of these groups is a divisive element that could tear apart the very spirit of our representative system, if they gain sufficient strength."

"Our lives begin to end the day we become silent about things that matter." —Martin Luther King, Jr.

35. BUILD A BIGGER TENT

Much of the Hispanic population is concentrated in five of the most politically powerful states—California, Florida, Texas, Illinois, and New York. These five states represent over 60% of the electoral votes needed to elect a president.

BACKGROUND. The days when blue-collar, ethnic, and immigrant voters automatically supported the Democratic party are long gone. But it's not because these voters don't agree with progressive policies any more; polls show that a majority do. It's just that Republicans have done an exceptional job of marketing their brand of right-wing "populism."

This is particularly true among Latinos, the fastest-growing segment of the electorate. One of our greatest challenges, if progressives are serious about winning elections again, is finding ways to reach them—and other groups of essential voters—with our *true* populist message and invite them into the Democrats' "big tent."

NEW POLITICAL POWER

• The Hispanic population is booming in America. According to the census, there were 23 million Hispanics in the U.S. in 1990; the latest estimate is 40 million, and it's suggested that by 2050 there will be 102 million—about 25% of the total population.

• Over the last 10 years, the Hispanic electorate has become swing voters. In 1996, they voted 73% to 21% in favor of Clinton. But eight years later, they voted 59% to 40% for Kerry—Republicans gained 20%. "No other constituency has shown such a propensity for changing candidates and parties," comments Sergio Bendixen, of the public-opinion consulting firm Bendixen and Associates.

• At first glance, this doesn't make sense. "Based on their day-to-day needs," says Jorge Mursuli, of People For the American Way, "you'd think Hispanic immigrants would be traditional Democrats. Most of the new generation is progressive about health insurance, schools, jobs, minimum wage.... And in foreign policy, they're internationalists; they believe in the U.N. and oppose the war in Iraq."

- So what's the Republican appeal? The GOP is better at outreach and communication. "Millions of Hispanics speak only Spanish," says Bendixen. "And even in homes where just one family member does, they often rely primarily on Spanish TV, local radio, and newspapers. The Republicans make sure everything they do is reported in Spanish-language media...but Democrats do little at the grassroots level. This is the Republicans' #1 advantage."

- "The Republicans also understand that this immigrant wave is different from any other," says Mursuli. "Many Latinos haven't given up their culture and assimilated...and they are easily influenced by candidates who seem to respect this."

SIMPLE THINGS YOU CAN DO

- For a long time, progressives have gone out of their way to be "inclusive." But we may have taken it to a point where it's counterproductive—where we're actually ignoring the unique qualities that are a source of pride and identity to many Americans. This has affected our ability to connect with all kinds of groups.

- How do we rectify that? In this case, suggests Mursuli, "get out of your comfort zone. Find out where your neighbors are from, why they came to America—what's their story? Be curious."

- Make Latin Americans in your city or county feel welcome. Establish contact thru neighborhood associations. Or get your organization to partner with a Latino group and sponsor pot lucks or picnics. "Republicans all over the country invite Hispanic small business-owners to lunch," Bendixen says. "We can certainly do the same."

- Make sure all news and notices of your group—including civic organizations and labor unions—are shared with Spanish-language media...in Spanish. While you're at it—if you speak Spanish, volunteer with your group as a bilingual blogger.

- Talk to progressive candidates about this issue. Get them in touch with Mi Familia Vota. Get them to develop thoughtful positions on immigration. And learn more about it yourself.

RESOURCES

- **Mi Familia Vota** (*www.mifamiliavota.org*)
- **Latinos for America** (*www.latinosforamerica.com*)
- **NDN's Hispanic Strategy Center** (*www.ndn.org/hispanic*)

Another good resource: Southwest Voter Registration Education Project (www.svrep.org)

THE WAR ON THE ENVIRONMENT

When you look at the outrageous environmental record of the Bush administration, you have to wonder: Aren't these people at all concerned about what will happen to their children and grandchildren? Three examples of their inexplicable, intolerable behavior:

A HOT ISSUE

In March, 2001, less than two months after taking office, President Bush shocked the world by ending U.S. participation in the Kyoto Protocol, a U.N. treaty that addresses the problem of greenhouse-gas emissions and their connection to climate change.

Shortly after, he requested a report from the National Academy of Sciences (NAS) to support his position that global warming is not a man-made threat. NAS's conclusion: "Greenhouse gases are accumulating in the earth's atmosphere as a result of human activities." The Bush administration's reaction: Ignore the report.

Since then, they've done everything they can to keep anyone from developing a plan to handle the issue. For example:

• In 2002, they got NASA's Robert Watson removed from the chair of the U.N. Panel on Climate Change. The reason: His outspoken stand on global warming antagonized the oil industry.

• In 2003, they eliminated the global warming section of the annual EPA Report because they didn't like its conclusions.

• In 2005, it was revealed that Philip A. Cooney, a White House aide who'd previously been an American Petroleum Institute lobbyist, had—for several years—been changing information in government climate reports, playing down links between emissions and global warming. He promptly resigned...and went to work for ExxonMobil.

THE ENDANGERED ACT

In 1973, Congress, with almost unanimous support, passed the Endangered Species Act (ESA) to protect plants and animals from

The Evangelical Christian Climate Initiative: www.christiansandclimate.org

extinction. It has been credited with saving hundreds of species, including the bald eagle, manatee, grey whale, and timber wolf.

Immediately upon taking office, the Bush administration began an attack on the act: They limited the number of species that could be listed; they reduced the designation of "critical habitat"; and they reduced Fish and Wildlife Service (FWS) funding for recovery programs.

Under President Clinton, 65 new species were added to the list every year. Under George W. Bush, the number dropped to 9.5.

Between 2001 and 2003, federal biologists recommended that 83 million acres of public land be listed as "critical habitat." The Bush administration designated less than half of that.

In 2005, the FWS estimated that about 200 currently-listed species were on the verge of extinction because there wasn't enough money in the budget to administer their recovery programs. So… the Bush administration cut even more of their funding for 2006.

THE CLEAN S**T ACT
Every year, rainstorms in the U.S. cause about 40,000 overflows of raw sewage at waste treatment plants. That sewage flows into streams, rivers, lakes, coastal waters—and basements of American homes. The Center for Disease Control reports that each year 8 million people are adversely affected by sewage-contaminated water, and 900 people die from illnesses related to exposure.

Shortly before he left office, Bill Clinton proposed new regulations to control the overflows, and require sewage facilities to notify the public when they occur. But as soon as George Bush became president, he put the project on permanent hold. It still hasn't been implemented. On top of that, in 2004 his administration cut $500 million from the Clean Water State Revolving Loan Fund—which gives communities money to repair aging sewer plants; it was nearly a third of their total funding. On top of that: The administration proposed a "sewage blending" plan that would have allowed treatment plants to discharge untreated sewage into the environment during storms after it had been "blended" with treated sewage. (In 2006, after massive public outcry they gave up on that one.)

"I think the environment should be put in the category of our national security. Defense of our resources is just as important as our defense abroad. Otherwise, what is there to defend?" —Robert Redford

36. PROTECT THE ENVIRONMENT

"George W. Bush will go down in history as America's worst environmental president." —**Robert F. Kennedy, Jr.**

BACKGROUND. It doesn't take much common sense to realize that if we pollute the air and poison the water, we're going to kill the planet...and ourselves.

Yet the Radical Right, working with the Bush administration, has been systematically undermining all of our environmental protections. Most Americans aren't aware of how much damage they've already done...and how much more destruction they're planning.

The single most effective thing we can do for the environment is to get the Radical Right out of power in Washington. Until then, it's up to us to spread the word about what's going on...and to support the grassroots groups that are fighting to protect what we still have.

WHAT WE'VE LEARNED

Our 1990 bestseller, 50 Simple Things You Can Do to Save the Earth, *focused on everyday actions people can take to protect the environment. But today, we need to do more.*

Spread the word. The Radical Right has shown such a shocking disregard for the environment, it's hard to believe. Learn everything you can about what they're doing, and pass it on. Google "Bush environmental record." Some sites to start with: Natural Resources Defense Council (*www.nrdc.org/bushrecord*), Greenwatch (*www.bushgreenwatch.org*).

Write letters to newspapers, businesses, politicians. Remind people that there's nothing "conservative" about the way the Right's plundering our resources. Stress the fact that the damage being done will affect our grandchildren...and their children.

Work in your community. A healthy environment is part of a healthy community. We all have a vested interest in a wetlands or stand of trees in our own backyard. And as we've mentioned elsewhere in the book, community action is nonpartisan—your politically conservative neighbor may be just as intent on saving a beautiful stream as you are. When you join forces, you set a precedent for the future.

• Support local environmental groups. Find them by Googling your area + "environmental group." Groups like the Sierra Club (*www.sierraclub.org*) may also have a local chapter.

• Show up at government hearings. Make sure someone from our side is there to speak up for the environment. (See p. 98.)

• The Rainforest Action Network organizes effective citizen action. Check out *www.ran.org*, and *www.jumpstartford.com*

Stay political. Individual actions like recycling and buying organic food are important...but they won't to keep coal plants from spewing mercury into the air. For that, we need laws—and politicians who are willing to fight for them.

• Get involved with pro-environment candidates running for local office. We cannot overstate the importance of supporting strong candidates at the local level. Help them make environmental protection a "wedge issue" against the Right. (See p. 110.)

• Contact your state League of Conservation Voters. Find out what candidates they're supporting...and what you can do to help. Start with the national Web site: *www.lcv.org*

• Contact your elected representatives: Demand that the government enforce the laws already on the books and tighten them where scientific advances show us new or different threats, and new opportunities.

MORE RESOURCES. An extensive list of environmental organizations: *www.nrdc.org/reference/environgroups.asp*

• A coalition of 19 major eco-groups, with links to each: *www.saveourenvironment.org*

• Download GoogleEarth for free (*earth.google.com*). Fly from outer space, right to your neighborhood, and gain a whole new perspective on what affects your local environment. Check out *www.nrdc.org/googleearth* and *www.sierraclubplus.org/arctic/maps/* to see examples of how environmental groups use GoogleEarth.

Democrats to the rescue! In 1987, Congress overrode Reagan's veto of the Clean Water Bill.

THE REAL
ECO-TERRORISTS

Trees? Clean air? Clean water? Who needs them?

Environmentalists are a socialist group of individuals that are the tool of the Democratic Party. I'm proud to say that they are my enemy. They are not Americans, never have been Americans, never will be Americans."

—Rep. Don Young (R-AK)

"Don't let anything like trees in the Clearwater National Forest get in the way of providing jobs and fueling the economy, even if that means cutting down every last tree in the state."

—Rep. Helen Chenoweth (R-ID)

"We know that acid rain has no significant environmental effect on trees or forests in the United States.... It is based on popular myths and half-baked theories."

—Haley Barbour, *then-GOP National Chairman*

"We are sick to death of environmentalism and so we will destroy it. We will not allow our right to own property and use nature's resources for the benefit of mankind to be stripped from us by a bunch of eco-fascists."

—Ron Arnold, *Center for the Defense of Free Enterprise*

"The EPA, the Gestapo of government, pure and simply has been one of the major claw-hooks that the government maintains on the backs of our constituents."

—Rep. Tom DeLay (R-TX), *ex-House Majority Leader*

"God says, 'Earth is yours. Take it. Rape it. It's yours.'"

—Ann Coulter, *pundit*

Oops! Criminal penalties for environmental crimes have declined 34% since Bush took office.

37. THE SPIN DOCTORS

"I admit it, the liberal media were never that powerful, and the whole thing was often used by conservatives as an excuse for conservative failures." —**William Kristol, The Weekly Standard**

BACKGROUND. Is news reporting biased? Of course it is. The news is just an interpretation of events. The question is, whose interpretation is going to reach the most people?

The Right claims the media is "liberal," but that's just part of their spin. We certainly know better. In fact, they do, too. The truth is, most journalists would just as soon get their story right, but often the information they get comes from a biased sources...and they're too busy to check. They also depend on people in power for scoops, which frequently means getting a right-wing slant.

Then there's the echo chamber effect: Once a story is reported, people often just repeat it without investigating for themselves. Soon the story takes on a life of its own—whether it's true or not. Saddam Hussein's "weapons of mass destruction" is a good example.

With their unlimited resources, right-wing groups like the Heritage Foundation and American Enterprise Institute can manipulate the media pretty easily. That's why it's so important to have people like you protecting our communities from excessive right-wing spin and making sure the progressive point of view isn't ignored.

SPIN DOCTORS

Here are three ways the right-wing point of view slips into the media:

• **Their "messaging" is adopted as legitimate communication.** The term "death tax," for example, was invented specifically to prejudice the public against the estate tax. It has no meaning except as a Republican talking point. Every time a newspaper uses it, they're unwittingly (or intentionally) promoting a political agenda. For an eye-opening perspective, check out Frank Luntz's playbook. (See p. 30 and "It's a Frame," p. 88.)

• **The right-wing echo chamber.** A group of far-Right outlets cooperate to force a story—often false—into the mainstream. It

"A barking dog is often more useful than a sleeping lion." —Washington Irving may start on the Drudge Report or in the *Washington Times* (an aggressively right-wing newspaper), then move to radio talk shows and FOX News. They'll repeat it so often and so insistently that eventually the mainstream media treat it like real news. A good example: the lie that Al Gore claimed to have invented the Internet—which was used to demolish his character in 2000, and may have cost him the presidency. Take a look at the original comment and see for yourself: (*www.snopes.com/quotes/internet.asp*)

• **Government propaganda** is passed off as news. Armstrong Williams, for example, was a columnist and talk show host. When he promoted the No Child Left Behind Act in the national media in 2004, he was taken seriously as an African American conservative with an independent voice. It turned out he was paid over $200,000 by the government to plug it.

SIMPLE THINGS YOU CAN DO

• Read your local newspaper (or watch local TV news, or listen to the radio), critically. Look for right-wing spin or any reporting that seems unbalanced. See if you can identify buzzwords and right-wing messaging. Write a letter to the editor pointing out the distortion and clarifying the progressive point of view. Do this as an individual or as part of a small group (see p. 92). A great resource for tips on what to look for: *www.causecommunication.com/forgetus/betterjournalism.html*

• **Research** (see p. 129). When you're not quite sure of the facts, use the Internet to look up details of an issue. Often you'll find the source of the "spin," the hidden agenda, and progressive perspectives to help you correct the record.

• **Adopt a journalist** or two, then track their reporting. Are they leaning right? How far; how frequently? Give them feedback; usually, you can find their e-mail addresses at the end of a story. Stay polite, informative, and impersonal.

• **Urge local media to sign up** with the Institute for Public Accuracy (*www.accuracy.org*). They'll get free access to highly qualified experts with a progressive point of view willing to be interviewed on news issues of the day. Research shows progressive voices are generally under-represented in the news.

38. POLL POSITION

According to an MIT/Caltech study, in 2000, 4 to 6 million Americans' votes were disenfranchised "due to faulty equipment, untrained poll workers, poorly designed ballots... or voter intimidation and suppression efforts."

BACKGROUND. Ever heard of a *poll watcher*? That's someone appointed by a political party or candidate to observe the voting on Election Day. Poll watchers are supposed to be there to guarantee that the vote is fair. But according to news reports, some have used their position to *undermine* democracy, harassing and intimidating minority voters in precincts that normally vote Democratic.

This is one of the ways the Republican culture of corruption has affected the democratic process. And it's one you can do something about. When there are honest poll watchers on the scene, there's less voter abuse. So...what are *you* doing on Election Day?

MAKING EVERY VOTE COUNT
• Working at the polls is a way to vote for democracy. You can help make sure that all eligible voters cast their ballot...and that can make a huge difference in a tight election. If someone had successfully assisted *just one more* disenfranchised Democratic voter in *only 10%* of Florida's voting precincts in 2000, Al Gore would have won the presidency.

• What are we up against? Here's an example: On October 21, 2002, Arkansas held a special election for U.S. Senate. In heavily Democratic Pine Bluff, five Republican poll watchers showed up at the polls and demanded photo ID from African American voters, and even photographed some of them. Both acts are illegal in Arkansas. Some voters stood their ground, but according to non-partisan observers, many were upset and left before casting their ballots.

Election Protection: In 2004, People For the American Way Foundation (PFAWF) and other organizations created Election Protection, a strictly nonpartisan program that trained 25,000 "Election

In 2004, Republicans sent 3,600 poll watchers to Ohio to challenge (mostly) black voters.

Monitors" to work in areas around the country where problems were likely to occur, focusing on minority voters. They helped voters locate their polling places, informed voters of their rights, recorded and reported irregularities.

SIMPLE THINGS YOU CAN DO

Be a Poll Watcher. Protect the integrity of the voting process by working inside a polling place as an observer on Election Day. Your presence will help prevent voter abuse.

• Democratic poll watchers also monitor voting lists to keep track of which Democrats haven't voted yet. During Election Day, they inform the local party. Democratic workers then try to contact people who haven't voted and help get them to the polls.

• Here's how to do it: You need to be *officially designated* as a poll watcher by a candidate or political party on the ballot, so call the local Democratic Party or a candidate's headquarters and set it up. Some states require preregistration; in others, you can simply show up on Election Day with authorization. Check with your voter registrar (listed in your phone book) to be sure, or call your local Democratic Party or League of Women Voters.

Be an Election Protection "Election Monitor."
There are two ways to do it:

1) Work with PFAWF. They'll train you over the phone or in person, then assign you to work in a target state. You pay your own transportation. Materials and meals are provided for Election Day.

2) Work on your own. Even if your state isn't targeted for a full monitoring program, you can create a volunteer opportunity close to home. After the training, PFAWF will supply you with a Voter's Bill of Rights for your state, and you can pick your own spot to work locally.

• **Another alternative:** Sponsor an Election Protection volunteer. It costs Election Protection $50 to train each Election Monitor so if you can't be one yourself, make a donation to sponsor someone else.

RESOURCE
• **PFAWF Election Protection:** Call 1-866-OURVOTE (1-866-687-8683). (*www.pfaw.org/go/election_protection*)

Nearly 80% of African American voters believe deliberate efforts are made to keep them from voting.

HERE'S WHAT *I* DO...

*Andrew Gillum is a disarmingly energetic and warm young man from Talla-
hassee, Florida. After graduating from college, he went job hunting...but
found that his days of political activism made it tough to find good employ-
ment. So he embraced his idealism...and started working to change America.*

When I was 23, I ran for the Tallahassee city commission.
People said I was too young, and I had no real financial
backing...but I won. It opened my eyes about what young
elected officials have to go through. Our struggle is different from anyone else's, because every time we open our mouths, we're under scruti-
ny—we get called 'that young person who just doesn't know any
better.' It's a real problem—you can go in with all the idealism in the
world, but if you get attacked or derided every day, eventually you're
going to say to yourself, 'I'm talented, why not go make some money
instead?'

"We know that 50% of our 21st-century governors and presidents
were elected to some office before the age of 35—there's an informal
pipeline that exists, that moves young officeholders into higher and
higher positions. So I began thinking, Why not invest the time and
resources in the young progressives you know are going to be the leaders? The Right does it—we need to, as well. So with the help of Young
People for the American Way Foundation, I created an organization
called The Young Elected Officials Network.

"The constituency I'm concerned about is people who should be
president, but they're not being welcomed into the process; they're not
anchored anywhere.... So we're beginning to network them together
in a system that gives them a chance to interact and helps them support each other. In January 2006, we brought 64 people together in
Washington, D.C., and attended workshops of all kinds. Now we plan
to have four progressive policy summits a year, in four regions of the
country—as well as monthly virtual town hall meetings, policy discussions, and leadership skills training.

"Anyone interested in putting this country on the right path should
contact us. If you know a young progressive who's holding, or running
for, office, tell them to contact me. We have to instill a village mindset
in this country again." Contact Andrew Gillum at *agillum@pfaw.org*

About 5% of elected officials are under 35...and about half of them are progressives.

LOONEY TUNES

Once comments like these were considered lunatic rants. Now they represent the views of many "mainstream" right-wingers. It's a chilling example of how extreme things have gotten in our country…and how important it is to get active, before America drifts so far right it never comes back.

Look, I lump liberals, communists, feminists, atheists, anarchists in one group—And to me they are TRAITORS."

—**"Patriotworld," blogger**

"When the culture is sick, every element in it becomes infected. While it is no excuse for this scandal [pederast priests], it is no surprise that Boston, a seat of academic, political and cultural liberalism in America, lies at the center of the storm."

—**Senator Rick Santorum (R-PA)**

"The modern Democrat is a traitor. They should be treated no differently than the Rosenbergs; tried in a court of law, convicted, and suffer the harshest punishment. Death by firing squad, preferably. On TV, if possible."

—**"The Modern Conservative," blogger**

"Oh, that America might see the last of these fish-eyed sacks of loathsome bile and infamy: Unwholesome in their birth; repugnant and stench-forming in their decline."

—**Tony Blankley, *Washington Times***

"Conservatives saw the savagery of 9/11 in the attacks and prepared for war; liberals saw the savagery of the 9/11 attacks and wanted to prepare indictments and offer therapy and understanding for our attackers."

—**Karl Rove, presidential advisor**

"Whether they are defending the Soviet Union or bleating for Saddam Hussein, liberals are always against America. They are either traitors or idiots."

—**Ann Coulter, author**

Originally our invasion of Iraq was called Operation Iraqi Liberation. Its acronym: OIL.

39. SUPPORT A BIG IDEA

*America spends $100 billion a year on foreign oil
...and another $100 billion simply protecting
our access to it in the Persian Gulf.*

BACKGROUND. One of the Right's persistent attacks on progressives has been that we have no proposals of our own; we just oppose Bush and the Republicans.

That's a lie...but it's been repeated so many times that many people have come to believe it. So we have to take it seriously.

The antidote? Big ideas; visionary proposals that embody the things we believe in. The Right has certainly mastered this concept. The fact that they continue to run for office touting "small government" without people laughing in their faces—given the size of Bush's budgets and deficit—should be enough proof that people respond to "big ideas," not details.

So how do we inspire Democrats to "think big"? Let's get behind one idea...and go from there.

THE APOLLO ALLIANCE

• In 1961, President John F. Kennedy asked Americans to get behind him on an outrageously ambitious project: By the end of the decade, he said, we'd put a man on the moon and return him home safely. Most people thought the Apollo Program was impossible, but Kennedy provided the resources and inspiration, and eight years later Neil Armstrong walked on the moon.

• Imagine a similar project today, focused on something much closer to home—energy independence. Well, there is one: The Apollo Alliance, named after Kennedy's ambitious program. It proposes to spend $300 billion over the next 10 years to rebuild our industrial infrastructure, depending on America's "can-do" spirit to take us out of the era of oil and into the inevitable era of alternative energy.

• The Alliance provides so many potential benefits that it's literally impossible to list them all here. Just a few examples: By investing in the project, America would become the leader in the world's most important new technologies; we would create millions of new,

What is patriotism? 66% of Americans say, "Driving a fuel efficient car is a patriotic act."

high-paying jobs; we'd have cleaner air; we'd reinvigorate our manufacturing base (think "auto industry") and national security would be strengthened (less dependence on foreign oil).

• The project has already been endorsed by all the major labor unions—Teamsters, AFL-CIO, United Steelworkers, etc....*and* major environmental organizations like Greenpeace, Natural Resources Defense Council, and the Sierra Club. These groups don't always see eye to eye. But along with many CEOs and business associations, faith-based organizations, and youth groups, they agree on the need for and benefits of the project.

• And the cost? An exhaustive economic analysis has determined that the Alliance would create three million jobs...and, because of the economic multiplier effect, would essentially pay for itself. That's what can happen if progressives get behind a single big idea.

SIMPLE THINGS YOU CAN DO

• **Join the Alliance.** Fill out a simple online form and get their newsletters and updates.

• **Take the Apollo Pledge.** Sign the pact to support the project in whatever way you can. And get your local members of Congress to sign the pledge as well. If we get a majority behind this, we can change the country—and the world—dramatically. If a candidate *won't* sign the pledge, it's a potential reason to vote against them.

• **Go to the Alliance Web site.** Find out what you can do locally. The Apollo national map will give info about how to get involved with local partners on legislation, ballot measures, and other efforts to move the Apollo vision forward in your state.

• **Get more involved in supporting alternative energy.** We all agree: There should be more alternative energy sources, but it's going to take grassroots activism to make it happen...starting with you.

RESOURCES

• **The Apollo Alliance** (*www.apolloalliance.org*)
• **The Energy Future Coalition** (*www.energyfuturecoalition.org*)
• **Alliance to Save Energy** (*www.ase.org*)
• **Natural Resources Defense Council's Reenergize America Campaign** (*www.nrdc.org/reenergize*)

I tell you, George Bush...He's just the right guy in the right place at the right time."—Sean Hannity

40. BE THE MEDIA

"As TV viewing habits migrate to the Web, we'll move from a tightly controlled media environment to an open one. Progressives must embrace this new culture; the future of democracy depends on it."
—Holmes Wilson, Participatory Culture Foundation

BACKGROUND. Every time you log onto the Internet, it should hit you: Mass communication has changed dramatically. Before the Web, the cost of reaching millions of people with information was prohibitive for anyone except huge corporations and groups. But today, anything is possible.

Of course, it's a challenge to go from being a consumer of news to assembling and disseminating it; not everyone wants to make the effort. But the point is, *anybody can.* If you're looking for a way to fight against the Radical Right's growing influence over the flow of information in our culture, here's something to consider.

A MODERN FAIRY TALE

• In the 1980s, a young man from Maryland gave up a string of dead-end jobs (7-Eleven clerk, grocery store clerk, phone salesman), moved to L.A., and got work in a TV-studio gift shop.

• In 1994, he began to post the Hollywood gossip he overheard at the shop on UseNet (early Internet discussion forums). After awhile the posts became popular, so he started his own Web site...and a few years later, he broke the story that almost brought down Clinton's presidency—the Monica Lewinsky scandal.

• The gift-shop manager with no journalism experience was Matt Drudge, whose Web site now reportedly averages about nine million hits a day. If he can do it, anybody can.

SIMPLE THINGS YOU CAN DO

• **Start a Progressive Blog:** Sure, there are plenty of blogs already, but that doesn't mean they're reaching everybody. If you start one, and the only traffic you get is friends and family, you can still be the hub that links them to big stories and perspectives they won't hear any other way. (Google "how to blog" for tips.)

• If you decide to blog, find out about your legal rights and how to

Is the Internet your primary source for news? Then, polls say, you probably voted for Kerry in 2004.

defend them. The Electronic Frontier Foundation has published a legal guide for bloggers: *www.eff.org/blogger*

• **Become a progressive podcaster:** A podcast is an Internet radio show that people can listen to on a computer or MP3 player. Major news outlets have podcasts, but millions of everyday folks like us make their own, too. Use free or inexpensive equipment (Google "how to make a podcast") to create a show that gets the progressive message out. Check out the "Blast the Right" podcast at *www.therationalradical.com*

• **Be a part of SourceWatch.org:** Created by John Stauber and Sheldon Rampton, authors of *Banana Republicans*. It's an online encyclopedia that, like Wikipedia, you can add to and edit—except that it's geared toward progressive issues. With so many people consistently adding to each subject, the entries grow deeper and broader all the time, and they can be a real resource when breaking news needs some follow-up info. There's a good chance thousands of people will read your article, because Google picks up individual entries from a "Wiki" and adds it to its index. So when users search on Google, they're likely to find what you've contributed. It's an easy way to have a real impact.

ANCHORS AWAY

• **Make your own news show.** Get a digital camera and report the real news. All you need is a computer with video editing software, and Internet access. There are plenty of sites with good instructions. Google "how to make your own internet TV." One example: *www.politicstv.com* (Another: *www.betterbadnews.tv*)

• **Get Democracy.** The Participatory Culture Foundation builds software that lets anyone with Internet access create their own virtual TV channel. Using *www.getdemocracy.com* you can broadcast your own video to hundreds of thousands of people at no cost, and also see what others have created.

• **Start a radio station.** Corporate media control is so widespread that local news and diversity of entertainment and information have been severely restricted. In response, hundreds of communities are creating low-power FM (microradio) stations. The Prometheus Radio Project serves as an advocate and resource (*www.prometheusradio.org*).

CHANGE IT!

If we want a competitive, public interest–oriented media system, we have to get involved in the crucial media policy debates that are going on right now.

OUR MEDIA SYSTEM ISN'T A FLUKE. It's the result of deliberate policies crafted behind closed doors by powerful corporations and high-priced lobbyists. From 1998 to 2004, Big Media spent more than $957 million on lobbying. The oil and gas industry, by comparison, spent $396 million in the same period. Consider the results:

• During the last 20 years, the number of corporations controlling a majority of media in the United States has dwindled from 50 to 5.

• In 1996, the largest radio owners controlled fewer than 65 stations; today, right-wing radio giant Clear Channel alone owns over 1,200.

• The U.S. spends just $1.49 per capita on public broadcasting—55 times less than the amounts spent by England or Germany.

Changing the system won't be easy. Large media corporations have extraordinary power. But citizens still have some influence. The decisions that shape the future of all media are being made right now in corporate boardrooms and the halls of Congress and the Federal Communications Commission. For too long, these policies have been made without our informed consent. If we want better media, we need better media policies. To get that, we must make our voices heard. Here are five things you can do:

1. GET INFORMED. Go to *www.freepress.net/squad.* You'll be able to get information specific to your interests, find people in your neighborhood who share your concerns, access tools for reform, and see what policy decisions are being made where you live.

• **Common Cause** (*www.commoncause.org*) can help you arrange a meeting with your congressperson.

• **Consumers Union** (*www.hearusnow.org*). Works to keep cell phone records private and cable rates low.

• **Center for Digital Democracy** (*www.democraticmedia.org*) offers provocative commentary on a wide range of media issues.

"We can fool some of the people some of the time...."

2. FIND OUT WHO OWNS YOUR MEDIA. The Center for Public Integrity's MediaTracker (*www.publicintegrity.org/telecom*) tells you which companies control the media in your town—and how much they're spending in Washington. Go to your local stations and ask to see the "public file" of complaints and comments from the community. If you add to the file, let them know you'll be contacting advertisers as well. Find out when their licenses are up for renewal, and time your complaints accordingly.

3. FILE COMMENTS WITH THE FCC. Big Media is trying to change the rules so that one company—like FOX News or Sinclair Broadcasting —can control up to three TV stations, eight radio stations and the daily newspaper in the same market. A public outcry stopped this scheme in 2003. But Big Media hasn't given up. FCC commissioners have promised to hold public hearings across the country on media consolidation. Be sure to turn out—support programming that is under assault from the Right. (See the schedule of hearings at *www.freepress.net/future* and visit *www.prometheusradio.org/media_activists_guide.shtml*)

4. KEEP THE PRESSURE ON IN CONGRESS AND ON THE CAMPAIGN TRAIL. Ask candidates to go on record with their positions on the media. This is important—the last time the Telecommunications Act was revised, legislators paved the way for the creation of Clear Channel and gave away billions' worth of the public airwaves to broadcasters. This time, the future of the Internet is at stake. (Don't know what to ask? See *www.freepress.net/action/tools/10questions.pdf*)

5. FIND A LOCAL MEDIA GROUP—OR START YOUR OWN. There are great groups working hard at the local level: San Francisco's Media Alliance (*www.media-alliance.org*), Oakland's Youth Media Council (*www.youthmediacouncil.org*), Seattle's Reclaim the Media (*www.reclaimthemedia.org*), and Philadelphia's MediaTank (*www.mediatank.org*), to name a few. Can't find a group near you, or want to start your own? Use the Free Press Action Squad to connect with other media activists in your neighborhood.

...and those are the ones we need to concentrate on."—George W. Bush

41. SUPPORT OUR TROOPS

*As of January 1, 2006, more than 30 Iraq and Persian Gulf War
veterans had entered congressional races across the country as
Democrats. Only one had entered as a Republican.*

BACKGROUND. You probably didn't expect to find this here.
The Radical Right has managed to convince America that
supporting right-wing politics is the same thing as supporting
our troops. That's a clever tactic—it earns them a lot of political capital and puts us on the defensive. But it's a lie.

It also hides their dirty little secret: In significant ways, the leaders of the Right have consistently turned their backs on soldiers, veterans, and military families.

Our challenge is to communicate to Americans that the Radical
Right is less patriotic—and the left is *more* patriotic—than they
think. One way to accomplish this is to support our troops and their
families in ways that reflect your genuine concern and make a real
difference in their lives.

ADDING INSULT TO INJURY
The leaders of the Radical Right have looked the other way while...

• The Bush Administration has scandalously failed to provide soldiers with armor and other protective equipment. Some soldiers in
Iraq have died because they didn't have body armor. Others have
been reduced to digging through landfills for scrap metal to use as
vehicle armor, or relying on family members to pay thousands of
dollars for state-of-the-art body armor the Pentagon failed to provide.

• The Bush administration repeatedly tried to shortchange veterans.
For example, at the same time they gave billions of dollars of tax cuts
to wealthy Americans, they underfunded veterans' health care by $2
billion in 2004 and $1 billion in 2005. It took a Democrat, Sen.
Patty Murray of Washington, to publicize and rectify the situation.

There are dozens of other examples of the Right's idea of "supporting
the troops." Check out Knight Ridder's articles on the subject:
*www.realcities.com/mld/krwashington/news/special_packages/veterans/
10991286.htm*

SIMPLE THINGS YOU CAN DO

The goal is twofold: Help our soldiers and express our patriotism. To inspire other progressives, be sure to identify yourself or your group as a Democrat or progressive in whatever you choose to do.

Support a soldier or vet directly: A lot of groups are working to make life better for active troops and vets returning from war. Pick one whose efforts you'd like to support. Contact local veterans' groups in your area for suggestions, or visit the groups listed below.

Raise money for the troops: Work with your group to organize a fund-raiser and use the money for soldiers or returning vets.

• Hold a dance, a car wash, a bake sale. Even if you raise only a few hundred dollars, you'll be able to purchase something meaningful, such as phone cards that enable soldiers to speak to their families. You can even collect used paperback books to send overseas.

• Include your organization's name in the event: e.g., "The Jackson County Democrats' Dance for the Troops." And include it in ads and flyers, too. Report the event to local newspapers.

• Invite a vet to speak at your local group meeting.

RESOURCES

• **Iraq and Afghanistan Veterans of America:** Nonpartisan advocacy group for Iraq vets; stays up to date on issues facing Iraq veterans. (*www.iava.org*) A list of "Troops Charities" is at *www.iava.org/index2.html*

• **The Fisher House Foundation:** Provides housing to family members of hospitalized soldiers. (*www.fisherhouse.org*)

• *www.AnySoldier.com:* Sends care packages to troops in Afghanistan and Iraq; Click on "What to Send" or "Where to Send."

• **Operation Uplink:** Provides soldiers and hospitalized veterans with free long-distance calling cards. (*www.operationuplink.org*)

• **Operation Hero Miles:** Collects unused frequent-flier miles for Afghanistan/Iraq soldiers or their families. (*www.heromiles.org*)

• **Soldiers for the Truth** (*www.sftt.org/main.cfm*)

• **National Gulf War Resource Ctr.** (*www.ngwrc.org/index.cfm*)

• **Gold Star Families for Peace** (*www.gsfp.org*)

• **Military Families Speak Out** (*www.mfsp.org*)

• **Iraq Veterans Against the War** (*www.ivaw.net*)

42. SEPARATION ANXIETY

"Religion and government will both exist in greater purity, the less they are mixed together." —James Madison

BACKGROUND. It's no secret that the Christian Right wants to impose their vision of a "Christian America" on us. Fortunately, our religious freedom is protected by the separation of church and state...or is it?

SEPARATED AT BIRTH?

• Fundamentalists like W.A. Criswell of Dallas's First Baptist Church are sure "there is no such thing as separation of church and state. It is merely a figment of the imagination of infidels."

• Most Americans disagree. In fact, polls show that 67% of us believe "separation of church and state" is in the Constitution.

• But here's a surprise: The phrase "separation of church and state" isn't. It's the *concept* that's contained in the religion clauses of the First Amendment, which read: "Congress shall make no law respecting an establishment of religion or prohibiting the free exercise thereof...."

A Matter of Judgment. Federal judges, supported by historical data and the writings of Jefferson and Madison, have determined that these two clauses express the Founding Fathers' intent to keep religion and government separate.

• But the Religious Right is still fighting it: "Our U.S. Constitution was founded on Biblical principles and it was the intention of the [Founding Fathers] for this to be a Christian nation," insists crusader David Barton. "If it was their intention to separate the state and church they would never have taken principles from the Bible and put them into our government."

• That's a bit far-fetched, since neither "Bible," nor "God," nor "Christianity" are even *mentioned* in the Constitution. But that doesn't stop the Religious Right. In 2002, for example, the Texas Republicans declared, "Our Party pledges to do everything within its power to dispel the myth of separation of church and state." What does that mean, exactly? Hopefully, we'll never find out.

Want an example of a government where there's no separation of church and state? The Taliban.

SIMPLE THINGS YOU CAN DO

• **Become an expert:** Learn the facts about separation and the Radical Right's arguments against it. Visit *www.wallbuilders.com*, Barton's Web site. Then go to *www.positiveatheism.org/writ/founding.htm* Compare the way the facts are presented; the key to arguing against the Right's view, you'll see, is understanding that they grossly misrepresent historical data.

• **Speak out:** People need to hear your point of view. If all they hear are the Religious Right's persuasive lies, the Right wins by default. Write letters to the editor. Donate books like *The Godless Constitution* to libraries. Support political candidates who are vocal supporters of separation.

• **Support national organizations:** Groups like Americans United for Separation of Church and State are leading the fight to protect American democracy. They depend on our support. Sign up for their e-mail alerts; become a member.

• **Be a watchdog:** Defend the Constitution in your community. For example: During an election cycle, you may notice a church overstepping its rights as a 501(c)(3) organization (i.e., a tax-exempt nonprofit) by endorsing a candidate. This isn't always intentional, so you may be helping them by pointing it out. If you need advice on how to approach them, contact a national group for assistance. Don't assume they know what's going on.

RESOURCES

• **Americans United for Separation of Church and State.** (*www.au.org*) Watchdog group to turn to for info and help.

• **The Constitutional Principle: Separation of Church and State.** (*members.tripod.com/~candst/toc.htm*) Great site.

• **The Baptist Joint Committee for Religious Liberty.** (*www.bjconline.org/index.html*)

• **Freedom from Religion Foundation.** (*www.ffrf.org/index2.php*)

• **Recommended reading.** *The Godless Constitution: A Moral Defense of the Secular State*, by Isaac Kramnick, R. Laurence Moore

• *Why the Religious Right Is Wrong: About Separation of Church and State*, by Rob Boston

What tradition? "In God we trust" didn't appear on U.S. paper money until 1957.

THE WAR ON SEPARATION

Most Americans consider the separation of church and state a fundamental part of our democracy. But the Christian Right is actively trying to undermine it—and they have an ally in George W. Bush. Already, more has been done to obliterate the church/state wall under this president than under any other chief executive in history. Don't like it? Too bad—Bush's "religion czar," Jim Towey, isn't interested in what he calls the "continued outcry from the secular extremists."

FAITH-BASED GOVERNMENT

In 2001, George W. Bush wanted Congress to pass a law establishing religion-based programs in the federal government. They refused. So in 2002, he issued an executive order establishing religion-based offices in 10 agencies (the Depts. of Justice, Labor, etc.).

Why? Bush claims he's trying to "level the playing field" so religious groups can get money to help needy Americans. But religious groups could already get government funds. The difference is, they had to operate under strict rules that forbade them from proselytizing or limiting hiring to employees of a particular faith or religious denomination. If Bush gets his way, religious groups will receive tax dollars for programs that hire only evangelical Christians. Already, for the first time ever, groups can take federal funds to renovate buildings that are used for religious worship. So your tax dollars may actually go into rebuilding the social hall at Jerry Falwell's church.

Political Payoffs? In fact, one of the first recipients of Bush's "faith-based" grants was Pat Robertson's Operation Blessing. It got $1.5 million...despite the fact that, as one critic points out, it had "recently been investigated by the state of Virginia for misusing relief funds to haul equipment for Robertson's for-profit diamond mining firm." And a Philadelphia church whose minister endorsed candidate Bush got $1 million. "Now there's a heavenly payoff," commented Barry Lynn of Americans United for Separation of Church and State.

"The great enemy of truth is very often not the lie...but the myth." —JFK

While many secular humanitarian organizations suffer cutbacks in funds, billions of dollars have been poured into the religious-based programs—$2.1 billion in 2005 alone. And in March 2006, Bush added an 11th faith-based office...in the Department of Homeland Security.

Ring of Ire

Meanwhile, hundreds of abstinence-only programs are run by faith-based groups, funded by your tax dollars. Is the real goal sex education...or prosyletizing? In Louisiana, the ACLU found that "thousands of dollars went to programs that included prayers as well as continuous references to God, Jesus Christ, and the spiritual repercussions of sex before marriage." Another case in point: The Silver Ring Thing, a traveling troupe that uses theater to teach "sexual purity"—which, they say, "can only be achieved by offering a personal relationship with Jesus Christ." When teens sign a "covenant before God Almighty" to remain virgins, they get a silver ring inscribed with a Bible passage reminding them to "keep clear of sexual sin." This group has received $1.5 million of our government's funds...and would have gotten more if the ACLU hadn't taken them to court for using "taxpayer dollars to promote religious content, instruction, and indoctrination." The Bush administration reluctantly withdrew its grants until the group revised its program.

THE GRAND CANYON REVISITED

The boundaries between church and state are being eroded everywhere. In 2003, Bush's deputy director of the National Park Service had three bronze plaques with quotes from Psalms 68:4, 66:4, and 104:24 installed on viewing platforms on the south rim of the Grand Canyon. The plaques were donated by a group of nuns who warn that an "avalanche of moral decay is upon us...our society is disintegrating." Their evidence: The removal of Judge Roy Moore's monument to the Ten Commandments in the lobby of the Alabama Supreme Court.

The superintendent of Grand Canyon National Park contended the religious messages violated the U.S. Constitution. But, as you might expect, he was overruled by the Bush administration.

In Florida, Gov. Jeb Bush dedicated the nation's first "religion-based prison."

43. START A
WEDNESDAY GROUP

*"If you want to say, 'Hey, guys, we'd like your help on an issue,'
there are 110 guys at the meeting," Mr. Norquist said.
"They come out of that meeting, go back to their groups,
and talk to thousands of people about it."*

BACKGROUND. Let's face it—turning the vast array of progressive interest groups into a unified political coalition sounds like a pretty daunting task. Yet it's critically important, because we can only win if we're unified.

Fortunately, someone has figured out how to do it. Unfortunately, that someone is a right-winger named Grover Norquist, whose ideas have helped create the coalition that rules the Republican Party. But there's a bright side: We can take his concept, modify it...and use it to fight the Radical Right.

THE WEDNESDAY MEETING

• In 1993, Norquist, head of Americans for Tax Reform in Washington, D.C., created a weekly Wednesday meeting to wage guerrilla warfare against the Clinton administration. About a dozen people showed up.

• A year later, there were 45 regulars—including representatives of the NRA, the Christian Coalition, and the Heritage Foundation. Today their mission has changed, and there are more than 100 members; even the White House is represented.

• Norquist has succeeded because he stays away from potentially divisive social issues and focused on political goals that all members can embrace. "There's no time for canned political rhetoric," writes Michael Scherer in *Mother Jones*. "The focus is on winning. Here, strategy is honed. Talking points are refined. Discipline is imposed."

• "What makes it work," says Scherer, "is an understanding that they'll *all* fight for the things that unite them, and each will get at least a small part of the things they want: Everyone gets something: If you don't get what you want now, your turn will come."

Grover Norquist Gets Candid: www.alternet.org/story/20448

SIMPLE THINGS YOU CAN DO

Duplicate Norquist's project on a local level (county, city, or town), creating a group that concentrates on strategic goals in your area. This is an invitation-only event designed to bring representatives of progressive groups together on a regular basis. It *is* a social event, but its real purpose is to create a movement by establishing a common political agenda and devising strategies to achieve it. Some practical tips:

1. Contact a few heavy hitters: Start with a few people whose involvement will lend credibility to the effort and help draw participants.

• Meet with them, make plans. Who leads the group? Who will its members be? Where will it be held? What's the agenda?

2. Make a wish list of participants: Identify allies, but remember, they don't have to agree on everything. Pick a minimum number of people to make it work. Let it grow from there.

• *Some possibilities:* Representatives from environmental groups, women's groups, trade unions, religious leaders, civil rights groups, teachers' organizations, artists and arts groups, alternative weeklies, prominent Democrats, elected officials, librarians, representatives from gay and lesbian organizations, reproductive-choice advocates (e.g., Planned Parenthood), progressive businesspeople.

3. Find a cooperation-building project: Start with a single goal or project that's acceptable to all (e.g., promoting a local land use law, tax reform, or school budget). Develop an agenda: goals, strategy, talking points, and a coordinated campaign to promote it...and fallback positions.

• The Right's political success evolved directly from this same spirit of cooperation. The progressive movement's success depends on it as well—and will benefit from it just as much.

RESOURCES

For more info on Norquist's meetings, check out these articles:

• "The Soul of The New Machine," by Michael Scherer. *www.motherjones.com/news/feature/2004/01/12_402.html*

• Many articles and links on Norquist and Wednesday Group meetings: *www.commonwealinstitute.org/information.html#weekly*

44. RELIGIOUS VOICES

According to Pew Research, 55% of Americans believe the Republican Party is pro-religion. Only 29% think the Democratic Party is.

B ACKGROUND. Pat Robertson likes to start sentences with the phrase "People of faith want..."
    If you're a progressive person of faith, you know there's little chance Robertson, a fundamentalist theocrat, has a clue what you want. Yet he and others like him have convinced the media—and much of the public—that they speak for all truly religious Americans.
    But you have the power to change this. All you have to do is speak up...and get others to speak up with you.

LEFT BEHIND?
• Don't underestimate the political power of your faith. When Democrats establish their identity as genuinely religious individuals, as Gov. Tim Kaine of Virginia did in 2005, they can neutralize one of the Right's chief weapons—the "moral-values" issue.
• That may be why the Right is doing all it can to undermine the Religious Left. Standard-bearers like Rush Limbaugh, for example, are constantly on the attack. "The Religious Left...hates and despises the God of Christianity," Limbaugh once told his listeners. He has also explained to his audience that liberals are "soulless," because "souls come from God."
• Limbaugh—and other right-wingers—have conveniently forgotten that, until the 1970s, religion was almost always invoked on behalf of liberal causes such as civil rights. In fact, the progressive movement would not exist today without the Social Gospel movement of the late 19th century.
• The secular Left may have forgotten this as well. "I literally have had liberals laugh in my face when I told them I was a Christian," says progressive activist Van Jones.
• This is a serious mistake. Some 85% of Americans consider themselves Christian, and about 95% believe in God. Religious voices must be an important part of the progressive movement.

Dear Pat: "You can safely assume that you've created God in your own image...

SIMPLE THINGS YOU CAN DO

Here are several simple ways to strengthen the Religious Left:

If you're a person of faith, speak up. By telling people at every opportunity that Robertson, Falwell, Dobson, and their ilk can't possibly represent all "people of faith"...because they don't represent *you*, you'll help transform America's view of religion.

• Challenge the Right on religious grounds: Progressives tend to argue in purely secular terms such as *It's a matter of privacy, It's a matter of civil liberties.* But we should also be arguing that there are competing *religious* values. Justice for everyone is a religious value, for example; so is equality.

If you're not a person of faith, welcome believers as a part of the progressive movement and encourage them to speak out. They're your allies. And their faith proves that liberalism is compatible with religious values.

Get liberal clergy involved. Encourage religious leaders to take a stand with you—people listen to them.

• Ask them to speak out. They can spread the progressive message by leading teach-ins and conferences, hosting gatherings, appearing on radio and TV. Get them to show up at town council and school board meetings to represent the progressive Christian or religious perspective.

• Get them to post their sermons on a Web site, or offer to transcribe them yourself and submit them as op-eds.

Join and support progressive religious groups. Progressive Christians have a special role in fighting the Right. Support the new online groups springing up to carry the banner of the Religious Left:

• **Cross Left:** *www.crossleft.org*
• **Crosswalk America:** *www.crosswalkamerica.org*
• **Center for Progressive Christianity:** *www.tcpc.org*
• **Progressive Christians Uniting:** *www.progressivechristiansuniting.org/index.shtml*
• **Christian Alliance For Progress:** *www.christianalliance.org*
• **Network of Spiritual progressives:** *www.spiritualprogressives.org*

For more religious resources, see page 86.

...when it turns out that God hates all the same people you do." —Anne Lamott

MAKE YOUR POINT

Sometimes, to really make your point, you have to argue. Here are some practical tips adapted from George Lakoff's Don't Think of an Elephant, *for those times when you do.*

S how respect.... No one will listen to you if you don't.... Listen to [the conservatives you're arguing with]. You may disagree strongly with everything being said, but you should know what is being said."

—"**Distinguish between ordinary conservatives** and nasty idealogues. Most conservatives are personally nice people, and you want to bring out their niceness and their sense of neighborliness and hospitality."

—"**Be calm.** Calmness is a sign that you know what you're talking about. Be good-humored. A good-natured sense of humor shows you are comfortable with yourself."

—"**Hold your ground.** Always be on the offense. Never go on defense. Never whine or complain. Never act like a victim. Never plead. Avoid the language of weakness—for example, rising intonations on statements. Your voice should be steady. Your body and voice should show optimism. You should convey passionate conviction without losing control."

—"**Expect...stereotypes, and deal with them** when they come up. Conservatives have parodied liberals as weak, angry (hence not in control of their emotions), weak-minded, softhearted, unpatriotic, uninformed, and elitist. Don't give them opportunities to stereotype you in any of these ways."

—"**By the way you conduct yourself, show strength,** calmness and control...a command of the basic facts; and a sense of being an equal, not a superior. At the very least you want your audience to think of you with respect.... In many situations, this is the best you can hope for. You have to recognize...that a draw with dignity is a victory in the game of being taken seriously."

"We must learn to treat leftists as natural disasters or rabid dogs." —Free Congress Foundation

45. RUN!

"If you already consider yourself an activist, it's not such a leap to think of yourself as a candidate. In fact, you might say it's a responsibility, an extension of the work you already do."
—**Gloria Totten, Progressive Majority**

BACKGROUND. There are a lot of people reading this book who'd make good mayors, school board members, judges, state legislators...even Members of Congress. You may be one of them.

So we'd like to ask you: Have you ever considered running for office?

Take the question seriously. Look around; many of the people holding office today are incompetent, self-serving...and right-wing. If someone like you doesn't challenge them, who will?

Granted, not everyone is cut out for elective office. But we need only a handful of successful candidates to lay the foundation for a strong progressive movement.

SHOULD YOU RUN?

Here are five things to ask yourself:

1. Do you have the temperament to run for (and serve in) office? "Once you declare your intention to run for office," writes Catherine Shaw in *The Campaign Manager*, "you become part of the public domain. You are fair game for just about any criticism people might...level at you." Can you put up with that?

2. Are you passionate enough about your principles to make a real effort, regardless of the outcome? "We need people who are committed to progressive principles, who are honest and authentic," says Gloria Totten. "People who passionately believe something already have a lot to offer as candidates."

3. Do you know know what you want to run for? Research the office: Find out who your constituency will be, what you'll do as an elected official, and what your legal obligations will be.

4. Do you have the qualifications for the job? What are your experience and skills? Are you already involved in your community? Do you belong to civic or political organizations? Do you

CPA State Action Blog: www.stateaction.org/blog

volunteer for causes like the PTA or the neighborhood watch?

5. Take a personal inventory. You need a strong support network to run. Do you have the time, family support, friends, name recognition (even if it's limited to the local school board), and public speaking skills needed for a good campaign?

SIMPLE THINGS YOU CAN DO

Contact Progressive Majority. If you think you might be interested in running, the first step is to call this group. They'll help you decide whether to run (and what to run for), then work with you to develop a professional winning campaign. In some instances, they can also help plan campaigns. It's a one-stop shop, fashioned after the Right's successful candidate development programs.

• **Get training.** Other groups train candidates as well. (See Resources.) We strongly recommend looking into this—politics is one place where training really matters. Don't try to do it alone.

• **Build your resume.** If you think you might run for office in the future, start joining your community, get experience, make a name for yourself.

Help recruit candidates. Do you know someone who'd make a great candidate? Someone who keeps popping up in local news…who owns a popular store or coffee shop…who's a good speaker, a natural leader? Tell Progressive Majority (or the other groups listed) about them. They're looking for our future leaders.

RESOURCES

• **Progressive Majority** (*www.progressivemajority.org*)
• **EMILY's List** (*www.emilyslist.org/do*)
• **Wellstone Action** (*www.wellstone.org*)
• **Grassroots for America** (*www.grassrootsforamerica.us*)
• **Democracy for America/Blog for America** (*www.DFAlink.com*)
• **United States Hispanic Leadership Institute** (*www.ushli.com/advanced_leadership*)
• **Dkosopedia:** A "how to run for office" section, with links. (*www.dkosopedia.com/index.php/how_to_run_for_office*)

Twelve "red" states have Democratic governors.

MILLENNIAL GENERATION

By 2008, 75 million people between the ages of 15 and 30 will be able to vote. If that includes you, check out these groups.

MUSIC FOR AMERICA (*www.musicforamerica.org*)
Mission: To engage young people in progressive politics through music and music communities. MFA has partnered with more than 325 bands at almost 4,000 concerts since 2003. Volunteers sign up online, go to free concerts, talk to friends and peers about political issues relevant to their lives, and register new voters.

• Text messaging, or SMS, via mobile phones, will be a factor in U.S. elections starting in 2006—and MFA will be leading it. Partnering with Mobile Voter, MFA is launching the TXTVOTER registration campaign, gearing up now for 2008.

CAMPUSPROGRESS.ORG (*www.campusprogress.org*)
Mission: To provide support for progressive voices on college and university campuses. Right-wing organizations spend millions each year on conservative groups at universities. Too often, progressive students have been left to fend for themselves. With Campus Progress Action Grants, students can fund progressive projects on campus, and its virtual meeting place, *CampusProgress.org*, gives students a chance to learn to communicate their values from people like Senator Barack Obama.

THE LEAGUE OF YOUNG VOTERS (*www.indyvoter.org*)
Mission: "To engage pissed-off 17–35-year-olds in the democratic process to build a progressive governing majority in our lifetime." They have more than 60 local groups in 21 states, and more than 1,500 volunteers speaking to young voters about progressive candidates. And their political action committee printed more than 350,000 local voter guides in key districts in 31 states.

CAMPUSACTIVISM. ORG (*www.campusactivism.org*)
Mission: To organize and link progressive student activists all over the country through their interactive Web site. They say their database has almost every American college and high school on it.

"Even fanatical Muslim terrorists don't hate America like liberals do."—Ann Coulter

46. ELECTION PROTECTION

In 2004, a 24-year-old hacker was able to "wreak havoc on the results" of a Diebold touch-screen voting machine using a flexible keyboard that was hidden in his shirt sleeve.

BACKGROUND. Some nations seem to have a hard time making democracy work. After a recent election in one country, for example, it was reported of the vote in just one province, that "more than 60,000 absentee ballots were never delivered, thousands of provisional ballots weren't counted, voting machines malfunctioned at polling places across the country, voters found themselves inexplicably removed from the voter rolls, and in some areas voters had to wait in line for hours before they were allowed to cast a ballot."

Was it in Kyrgyzstan? Nigeria? No. It was the 2004 U.S. presidential election.

DID YOU KNOW...

• There are many problems with U.S. elections, but the biggest long-term threat to democracy today is "black-box" computerized voting machines, which have no paper trail and can be "hacked" with ease, by anyone who knows the program." If these machines become the standard for American voting, no one will ever be sure whether election results are accurate...and our elections will be total shams.

• This is not speculation. We already know the machines aren't accurate. In the last presidential election there were thousands of complaints in at least 21 states. Voters complained that the machines consistently flipped Kerry votes into Bush votes. In Clearwater, Florida, for example, one woman had to recast her vote 10 times before the machine would count it for Kerry rather than for Bush.

• We also know that they can be hacked—which means someone can alter the results without a trace. Diebold, the manufacturer has claimed this is impossible. But on December 13, 2005, a Finnish

Must read: Mark Crispin Miller's book, *Fooled Again: How the Right Stole the 2004 Election.*

security expert did a test on a Diebold machine in Florida. He was able to change the result of a "test election" from a 6-to-2 "no" vote to a 7-to-1 "yes" vote.

• This is not a partisan or left/right issue, but a civic issue of profound importance.

SIMPLE THINGS YOU CAN DO

• **Get involved locally.** Learn more about how elections are conducted in your area. Meet your local election officials.

—Some states have an election reform organization (e.g., the California Election Protection Network). Contact the group in your state and work with them. Find them on Google or contact: *votersunite.org* or *blackboxvoting.org* for information.

—Try to observe pre-election testing—sometimes called "logic and accuracy testing." Every county tests voting machines, and the public can usually observe. Call your county election office about two months before the election. (You can also observe vote counting after the election.) Officials are more careful when people are observing. For more information, contact the resources below.

• **Become a poll worker.** They're always needed and are crucial to a smooth local election. You'll be there to help, but also as an observer, to make sure things are on the up and up. Contact your county registrar of voters for information on how to sign up.

• **Work to help pass federal legislation.** (See Resources below.) Remember to treat it as a bipartisan issue. Both Republicans and Democrats can be helpful…or obstructionist.

• **Spread the word.** Until the American people learn what really happened in the last election (and what's been happening since), true reform will be impossible. Do all you can to tell your fellow citizens the facts—and force the media to report such news consistently and clearly.

RESOURCES

• **Voters Unite:** (*www.votersunite.org*)
• **Verified Voting:** (*www.verifiedvoting.org*)
• **Black Box Voting:** (*www.blackboxvoting.org*)
• **Election Line:** (*www.electionline.org*)

The secret of success? Turnout is considerably higher in countries that vote during weekends.

PROTECTING RELIGIOUS FREEDOM

The Far Right justifies its relentless assault on religious liberty in America with its contention that the U.S. is a "Christian nation." You—and many on the Right—probably don't know that in one official document, our government explicitly declared that it isn't. Here's the story.

In 1797, our government signed a document called the "Treaty of Peace and Friendship between the United States of America and the Bey and Subjects of Tripoli, or Barbary," commonly known as the Treaty of Tripoli. Article 11 of the treaty includes this:

> As the Government of the United States...is not in any sense founded on the Christian religion—as it has in itself no character of enmity against the laws, religion, or tranquillity of Musselmen [Moslems]—and as the said States never have entered into any war or act of hostility against any Mehomitan nation, it is declared by the parties that no pretext arising from religious opinions shall ever produce an interruption of the harmony existing between the two countries.

No one knows exactly how Article 11 wound up in the treaty—there's no record of the negotiations—but in the end, what really matters is the reaction it received.

"The document," writes Brooke Allen in *The Nation*, "was endorsed by Secretary of State Timothy Pickering and President John Adams. It was then sent to the Senate for ratification [where it was read on the floor]; the vote was unanimous. It is worth pointing out that although this was the 339th time a recorded vote had been required by the Senate, it was only the third unanimous vote in the Senate's history. There is no record of debate or dissent. The text of the treaty was printed in full in the *Philadelphia Gazette* and in two New York papers, but there were no screams of outrage, as one might expect today."

"Every lesbian spear-chucker in this country is hoping I get defeated."—Rep. Bob Donana (R-CA)

HERE'S WHAT *I* DO...

What happens when you're the only Democrat in your house...and your parents don't know it? Here's what 17-year-old Teddy Gambordella, a high-school junior in Highland Park, Texas, did.

TEDDY'S TALE: "For 17 years, I've been indoctrinated daily by my father with Republican politics—I've spent hundreds of hours listening to Rush Limbaugh, and thousands of hours listening to my dad berate and belittle every Democrat, alive or dead.

"But by doing some independent research and a lot of independent thinking, I found that the Right is wrong on most things. However, I wasn't prepared for the consequences of my telling my father I was joining the dreaded Democrats.

"It occurred during the holiday season in 2005, when we were discussing Katrina and the damage to New Orleans. I was appalled by the government's response; I said more could have been done, quicker and better—but my father saw it just the other way. This led to a discussion of my political views, and I told him I was determined to become—and stay—a Democrat. His reaction was immediate and loud: 'Why in the world would anyone want to become a Democrat? I can't think of a single reason!' When I replied I could think of a million reasons, he said, 'Prove it.' So I started a Web site: *www.onemillionreasonswhy.com*

"I began my research by simply typing 'reasons to hate Bush.' I was overwhelmed with 800,000+ Web pages full of millions of reasons not to like Bush and the Republicans. So I knew I was on to something.

"Then my father told me that if I became a Democrat, he wouldn't pay for my college, so I thought I would use the Web site to raise money to pay for it.... Please let me say I love my father; he's my best friend, and we're not 'enemies' because of my becoming a Democrat. My father says he isn't doing this to punish me, but to teach me a lesson. His lesson: The Democrats won't support me, I won't be able to get a million reasons, and I won't be able to raise any money for college. I intend to stay the course and prove him wrong. All I need is publicity, because I know there are millions of Democrats who do want to help me and who agree with me."

For information about Teddy's project, check out his Web site at
www.onemillionreasonswhy.com

"My answer is, bring them on."—President George W. Bush

47. STANDING ON COMMON GROUND

At every U.S. Conference of Mayors annual meeting, Republican and Democratic mayors join forces and spend one morning working with Habitat for Humanity, building new homes for low-income families.

BACKGROUND. Sometimes the only way to defeat the Radical Right is to stand up to them. But other times, the best way to win the fight is not to fight at all.

When it comes to building a strong community, for example, the best tactic is cooperation. Why? The anti-democratic Radical Right, as we've pointed out, thrives on polarization; when there's a "good guy" and a "bad guy," they're in their element. So creating trust, respect, and cooperation between neighbors isn't just a progressive value—it's a way to undermine political radicals.

One good way to begin building bridges with your conservative neighbors is to join forces on a community-improvement project.

JOINING FORCES

• During the late 1980s, a nonprofit called the Giraffe Project was hired to bring together the conservative Republicans and politically left "hippie" residents of Carmel, California. It was a seemingly impossible task; traditional methods like public meetings led only to more tension. There was only *one* thing both sides agreed on: They loved Carmel. So Giraffe leader John Graham organized a "Clean Up, Fix Up" day. Volunteers from both sides worked together in small groups to beautify the town. "It was a breakthrough," recalls Graham. "They began to see each other as individuals instead of political and cultural enemies. A lot of strong relationships were built by that project."

• In 2000, in Ashland, Oregon, two families—one staunch liberals, the other conservative Republicans—joined forces to turn an unused building into a hands-on science museum that would benefit the community. "Politics was never the focus—it was all about doing something for Ashland," says one of the lefties. "Once

"The impersonal hand of government...

we were a team, working toward a common goal, politics became just another topic of conversation…and a way to razz each other. I don't think the mutual respect we developed could ever be dislodged now by mere political differences."

SIMPLE THINGS YOU CAN DO

Join an ongoing activity. *Two examples:*

• **Habitat for Humanity** (*www.habitat.org*). Build low-cost houses alongside the future owners. They have 1,500 affiliates in the U.S.

• **Rebuilding Together** (*www.rebuildingtogether.org*). One day a year, teams of people volunteer to improve life for needy people.

Create an activity. *There are plenty of community improvement activities you can start that have been successful elsewhere. For example:*

• **Adopt a park.** If your Parks and Rec. Dept. doesn't already have one, talk with neighbors about starting an "adopt-a-park" program. Groups like Austin Parks Foundation, Austin, TX (*www.austinparks.org*); Partnerships for Parks NYC (*www.partnershipsforparks.org*); and Neighborhood Parks Council, S.F., CA (*www.sfneighborhoodparks.org*) help maintain and even enhance local park facilities. There are many more; just Google "neighborhood parks groups."

• **A block-cleaning party.** Clean up yards and common areas like streets, sidewalks, and storm drains; help each other by sharing yard tools and cleaning supplies; organize trips to the local dump or landfill. For info on planning a one-day volunteer event, visit *www.pointsoflight.org/resources* (also see their Neighboring Program *www.pointsoflight.org/programs/neighboring*).

• **A neighborhood watch program.** Protecting each other builds solidarity. For ideas and guidelines, Google "neighborhood watch program."

RESOURCES

To find community-improvement volunteer opportunities in your area:

• **Newspapers:** Most list community projects in their "Volunteer Opportunities" section—both online and in print.

• **Volunteer Match:** Helps you find volunteer opportunity in your area. (*www.volunteermatch.org*)

• *www.local.com*: Type keywords "volunteer community projects."

…can never replace the helping hand of a neighbor." —Hubert H. Humphrey

48. JOIN THE PARTY, PART II

There are about 175,000 precincts in the USA. To win consistently, the Democrats need a presence in every single one.

BACKGROUND. If you think it's important to revitalize the Democratic party, and you've got some time to volunteer, why not consider becoming a precinct captain in your area? As part of the Democratic "establishment," you'll be in a position to influence the direction of your local party while doing important work—organizing voters to defeat the Right at the polls.

POLITICS 101

What's a Precinct? To make voting manageable, every county in America is carved into small geographic units called precincts. The size of a precinct is based on how densely populated an area is. It usually contains 200 to 1,000 people and at least one polling place.

What's a Precinct Captain? The Democrats have a volunteer organization in each precinct; the person in charge is the precinct captain (PC). "Your job," explains the San Francisco Democratic Party in its PC how-to manual, "will be registering neighbors to vote, as well as encouraging voters to get involved with community activities and to support Democratic Party issues and candidates."

Who Can Be a PC? Anyone. No experience is needed. All it takes is a willingness to work and a desire to see Democrats get elected. Most local party organizations will train you, so it's easy to learn.

Why Is a PC Important? PCs are the face of the Democratic Party at the grassroots level. They work with individual voters, building the party in their neighborhood. And when Election Day arrives, they're responsible for getting Democrats to the polls. Elections are won and lost on the ground. In a tight race, the party with the best organization is likely to come out on top. An active, committed PC can make all the difference.

Based on current fiscal policy, U.S. Treasury bonds will be "junk bonds" in 2026.

Is Precinct Captain an Official Democratic Position? Yes. In most states, the chain of command goes from PC to PC Coordinator (in charge of several precincts) to county chair. County chairs are on the state committee, which elects a state chair. So PCs are an important part of the party infrastructure. "If you're interested in reforming or giving input to the Party," says one experienced PC, "it's a great place to start."

SIMPLE THINGS YOU CAN DO

Follow these Three Steps: (1) Find out what precinct you're in. Your local election office will know. (2) Contact your local Democratic party for info. Ask what precinct captains do (including what they're called in your area). Are they elected or appointed? Is there already one in your precinct? (3) Volunteer to become a precinct captain…or to help one.

• There's no one-size-fits-all way to become a PC. Each local party is different: Some recruit directly online; some publish how-to handbooks; some refer you to a volunteer coordinator.

• Be patient; be persistent. Ironically, although PCs and other volunteers are desperately needed by the Democrats, it may take several e-mails or phone calls before you find the right person to make it happen. Some party chapters are very organized; others have a power structure that's been in place since JFK, and it can be hard to inject new blood. But keep trying. They do need you.

RESOURCES

Here are four articles to inspire you to become a precinct captain:

• **Chris Bowers** of the MyDD blog becomes a committeeperson (precinct captain) in Philadelphia. Read about his experience: *www.mydd.com/story/2005/11/29/133241/03*

• **The San Francisco Democratic Party** explains a PC's job. *www.sfdemocrats.org/sfd/captain_info.html*

• **The Washington Democrats'** handbook for precinct committee officers: *www.seattlewebcrafters.com/wspco/index.shtml*

• **The Practical Progressive Activist:** "Why You Should Become a Precinct Chair." *practicalactivist.blogspot.com/2005/03/why-you-should-become-precinct-chair.html*

THE WAR ON PUBLIC LANDS

"I don't see any justification for the federal government owning land, other than the Statue of Liberty and maybe a few parks, maybe a few refuges. But to just own land to do nothing with it I think is a disservice to the Constitution." —Rep. Don Young (R-AK)

WOOD YOU DO IT?
In 1905, President Theodore Roosevelt established the U.S. Forest Service and created the modern national forest system. One hundred years later, writes the *Los Angeles Times*, "the Bush administration has laid out plans to sell off more than $1 billion in public land during the next decade.... Experts said [it] would amount to the largest sale of its kind since the U.S. Forest Service was created. 'This is a fire sale of public lands. It is utterly unprecedented,' said Char Miller, a professor who has written extensively about the Forest Service.'"

WHO NEEDS 'EM?

When the National Park Service was created in 1916, Congress declared that its official goal was to "conserve the scenery and the natural and historic objects and the wild life therein" and to "leave them unimpaired for the enjoyment of future generations."

The park system has been run with that mandate in mind...until now. With the Bush administration's cooperation, Paul Hoffman, an anti-environmentalist who serves as our deputy assistant secretary for Fish, Wildlife and Parks, has begun rewriting the mission of the national parks. What are his qualifications? From 1985 to 1989, the former head of the Cody, Wyoming, Chamber of Commerce was the Wyoming state director for then-Rep. Dick Cheney. That's it.

"Hoffman," says the *LA Times*, "wants to upgrade grazing and mining to 'park purposes,' allow cell-phone towers and low-flying airplanes within national parks, and allow snowmobiles on all paved roads in every park. In addition, he wants to take away the park managers' abilities to use laws such as the Clean Water Act and the Clean Air Act to protect the parks from development. Finally, he wants to deemphasize dark skies and quiet even though they are conditions needed by wildlife."

J.T. Reynolds, the superintendent of Death Valley National Park, is appalled. "They are changing the whole nature of who we are and what we have been," he told a reporter. "I hope the public understands that this is a threat to their heritage. It threatens the past, the present and the future. It's painful to see this." For more info: *http://www.newwest.net/ index.php/main/article/4542*

HISTORICAL FICTION

The Lincoln Memorial, in Washington, D.C., is run by the National Park Service. "Since 1995," reports the *Washington Post*, "the interpretive center at the Lincoln Memorial has shown an 8-minute long film depicting various demonstrations and gatherings at the monument, including anti-war protests, concerts, and Martin Luther King's most famous speech."

Not any more. "The Park Service has bowed to pressure from the Religious Right to rewrite the history of protests on the national mall. Last month, the Park Service bowed to demands from Christian groups to edit out footage of anti-Vietnam War protests and images of gay rights and pro-choice demonstrations…. The Park Service HQ responded that they would edit the film to present a "more balanced" version. The new film will included footage of rallies by anti-abortion and Christian groups, such as the Promisekeepers, and shots of a pro-Gulf War demonstration. Neither of these events took place at the Lincoln Memorial."

HOLY ENDANGERED SPECIES!

According to the NRDC, "The Bureau of Land Management, caretaker of more land and wildlife than any federal agency," has a new policy: They keep their own biologists from monitoring wildlife damage caused by energy drilling on federal land, and spend money earmarked for conservation on—what else—energy. "They are telling us that if it is not energy-related, you are not working on it," complains a biologist. Scientific studies show worrisome declines in wildlife around gas fields, but that's not slowing down the BLM. They're frantically issuing permits to drill in Wyoming, "even though the oil and gas industry…can't drill nearly enough holes in the ground to keep up with the permits that have already been granted."

"The nation that destroys its soil destroys itself." —Franklin D. Roosevelt

49. "IT'S THE STATES, STUPID"

The federal minimum wage hasn't been raised since 1997 because Republicans oppose it...so progressives have begun concentrating on raising state minimum wages instead. Since 2004, twelve states have hiked their minimum wage, and more will do it in the near future.

BACKGROUND. "People have a sense that right now Democrats are completely powerless in Washington, that they're just sort of bystanders," says Charlie Cook, editor of the nonpartisan *Cook Political Report*.

No wonder. Republican legislators rarely let Dems get bills to the floor...and when they do, the press doesn't pay much attention. For example: Did you know that Sen. Ted Kennedy introduced legislation to increase the federal minimum wage in October, 2005? He lost in a close vote, 51 to 47, but hardly anyone heard about it.

So how are we going to convince America that progressive programs really work if we can't get any of them passed...and no one seems to know we're even trying?

How about shifting the focus from Washington to the states? By working in state legislatures and through ballot initiatives, we can bypass the federal government and create laboratories of democracy to prove that progressive programs work. This will not only help millions of people, but demonstrate what we can accomplish when we finally get the chance to control policy on a national level.

DID YOU KNOW...

• Democrats have power in the states. They control 22 governorships, and hold at least one of the Houses in 28 states.

• Working in the states plays to progressives' main strength—grassroots activism. Even a small numbers of people mobilized at the state level can have considerable influence. And while progressives are always outspent by the Right, it takes relatively little money to have an impact in states with ads, lobbying, etc.

Political training ground: 57% of congressmen and 44% of governors once served as state legislators.

• As it turns out, plenty of progressive issues besides minimum wage hikes play very well in the states. For example:

—**Fair Share Health Care.** Requires a state's largest businesses to spend a minimum percentage of their payroll on workers' health care costs, relieving taxpayers of that burden. In Maryland, where it has 80% approval, the legislature overrode the governor's veto and passed it. It's being introduced in other states as well.

—**Using public pension funds for economic growth.** States hold a total of $2.7 trillion in pension fund assets. Rather than being used for corporate welfare, these *could* be used to promote local, sustainable economic growth, affordable housing, and good business practices (rewarding companies that pay a living wage, offer health care, etc.).

—**Contraception issues.** Should rape victims have automatic access to emergency contraception? There's overwhelming public support for the idea, but Right-dominated state legislatures say no. It's a wedge issue that shows progressives are in the mainstream of American politics.

SIMPLE THINGS YOU CAN DO
Find out what's going on in your state:

• **Check out the Progressive Legislative Action Network** (PLAN). To find out about local legislation and the groups working on it, visit their Web site: *www.progressivestates.org*

• **Contact the Ballot Initiative Strategy Center.** Their goal: "Bring together…groups committed to…ballot initiative campaigns, to strengthen progressive politics and policies across the states." They'll tell you who to contact to work on ballot initiatives in your state. (*www.ballot.org*)

• **Contact the Center for Policy Alternatives** (*www.cfpa.org*). Provides tool kits to help legislators and activists pass state legislation. Lists progressive lobbying groups and connects you to state legislators. Go to their home page and click on "progressive directory." Another contact: state PIRGs (Public Interest Research Groups): *www.pirg.org*

• **Contact your state's chapter** of a national organization like the ACLU or Sierra Club to see what they're working on in your area.

A plan to fight the Right in the states: *www.progressivestates.org/content/57/governing*

50. GET ON THE BUS

In 2004, volunteers with the Bus Project knocked on 8,000 doors for a few state senate candidates in Washington state. One of them won by 600 votes, Democrats took control of the state senate, and Washington was able to pass groundbreaking new civil rights legislation.

BACKGROUND. In 2001, a group of young activists in Oregon decided to find a solution to a common campaign problem: How can regular citizens impact elections...even without lots of money to donate? Studies show that person-to-person contact is effective...but how can you find enough volunteers to canvass where it counts—in competitive areas where a few more workers might tip the balance? After several "cocktail-napkin-centered discussions" and months of organizing, the group launched the Bus Project, a unique mobile political-outreach organization.

WHAT THEY DID

• Their resources were limited so they carefully selected strategic races to work on. "We got voter data from the State Office of Elections," says the project's founder, Jefferson Smith. "We examined registration, voter performance, and whether an area had a tradition of close elections."

• Next, they filed as a political action committee with the Secretary of State—"which, it turns out, wasn't too bad."

• Then they bought a bus. "As a symbol," says Smith, "it evokes images of the Freedom Riders, Rosa Parks, Ken Kesey; it's also a good metaphor—'Get on the bus,' 'Don't miss the bus.'" Practically speaking, a bus is an ideal to way to bring 50 people to an area for canvassing, and it's a great way to build community. On the way, people meet one another and talk politics.

• By 2002, the Bus was ready to roll. They traveled all over Oregon, knocking on nearly 70,000 doors, doing service projects, and talking to people on behalf of progressive candidates and issues. In 2004, the Bus rolled again; this time the group knocked on 100,000 doors.

In studies on voter turnout, paid phone-callers had no impact, while volunteer phone-bankers...

- In those two elections, the Bus supported 10 state senate candidates in close races….and 9 won, helping Democrats gain control of the Oregon senate for the first time in over a decade.

- One of their key goals was to attract young people by "injecting fun and zaniness" into local politics. With events like the Hip-Hop Voter Drive and beer-filled issue forums, the Bus Project registered thousands of new voters for the 2004 election.

- The Bus now has thousands of volunteers who organize house parties, concerts, conventions, a summer institute, and voter outreach programs …"all to put the progress in progressive—not just left or right, but forward."

SIMPLE THINGS YOU CAN DO

- Start your own Bus Project. The folks in Oregon are eager to work with you. They'll provide tips, guidance, and inspiration.

- If you don't want to buy a bus, you can adapt their project so it works on a smaller scale. "We can help people to do one of our mini-programs," Smith explains—for example, a single mass canvass: With 50 people, you can knock on 2,500 doors on a Saturday. Each person gets a "walk list" (a walking map of the area they should go to) and is assigned between 40 and 75 doors. And don't forget the party afterwards.

- The Bus has a unique canvassing technique they call the "Listening Canvass." "Instead of *selling* ideas," Smith explains, "we ask for them. (Typical question: 'If you had one idea or issue you'd want the candidate to bring with them to the statehouse, what would it be?') And then we deliver that info to help the candidate, so they can build an unmatched connection to voters in the district. We also collect e-mails so the candidates and voters can stay in touch."

- The most important thing you may be able to pick up from Smith and his crew is their sense of fun and creativity. They've come up with some astoundingly effective ways to reinvigorate the democratic process…and have a blast at the same time.

RESOURCE

- **The Bus Project:** (*www.busproject.org*)

178

...increased turnout by 2-5%. And door-to-door canvassing increased turnout by 12-15%.

UP AND COMING...

The progressive movement is growing fast; there's always something under the radar, about to emerge as an influential force. For example:

Civic Footprint (*www.civicfootprint.org*). The Center for Neighborhood Technology (*www.cnt.org*) has developed the Civic Footprint so citizens can figure out how to stand up for the issues that impact their lives. It currently provides users in the Cook County area (Chicago and its environs) easy access to scattered, and therefore underused, data—everything from a personalized list of elected representatives to their police beat and judicial subcircuit. This is a great model to replicate. Plans include geographic expansion and the introduction of "cool mapping tools."

GoodStorm (*www.goodstorm.com*). Want a way to raise money for your organization that will cost you nothing and require little effort? We thought so. GoodStorm's founders set out to create an easier and more sustainable way for progressive groups and campaigns to support themselves—without needing a great deal of money, time, or expertise. The result: a free service that lets individuals, groups, and organizations open online stores stocked with items they design. The kicker? An incredible revenue share: 70% to the partner/storeowner and 30% to GS. They've even figured out how to work with PACs and (Democratic) political campaigns, so you can turn your creative political product into a powerful fundraising tool for your favorite progressive candidate.

New Progressive Coalition (*www.newprogressivecoalition.com*). A matchmaking service for the emerging Left, "working to wire progressive politics." By introducing investors and experts to political organizations, NPC is knitting together a vibrant network that strengthens the progressive movement. Using NPC's site, investors, political action groups, nonprofits, and start-ups can exchange ideas and resources of all kinds, and share the important lessons learned from their experiences. Membership (nominal fee) provides exposure to exciting political ventures across the country, as well as professional advice to help you find or become the next MoveOn.org.

"I'm the commander—see, I don't need to explain—I do not...

STATE OF THE UNIONS

"The most successful anti-poverty, middle-class-building, equal-opportunity, pro-community program in the United States is called 'unions.' Every progressive has a responsibility to support working people who are trying to form, strengthen, and modernize unions." —**Andy Stern, president, Service Employees International Union (SEIU)**

THE RIGHT TO UNITE. Polls show that more than 50 million Americans would like to have a union where they work, yet only 13 million do—and the number is dropping. Why? The corporate-backed Right has weakened labor laws to the point that companies can freely fire and intimidate workers who unite to improve their jobs. When corporations are faced with employees who want a union, 92% require them to attend anti-union meetings with the management that controls their working conditions, assignments, and chances for promotion.

LIBERTY AND JUSTICE FOR ALL. When 1/3 of American workers were in unions, union companies set the standard in our economy—establishing benefits such as health coverage, paid time off, and pensions. Today, major backers of the Right include anti-union Wal-Mart, which, as the largest employer in the world, sets everyday low standards for pay and benefits. The average wage at Wal-Mart is below the poverty line for a family of three, a majority of employees are not covered by the company's health plan, and none receives a pension. (By comparison, average pay at Costco is 65% higher than at Wal-Mart.) More than 70% of Wal-Mart products are made in China by workers paid as little as 25¢ an hour. The company has driven hundreds of other U.S. businesses to shift operations to China to keep their Wal-Mart supply contracts.

THE VOTING DIFFERENCE. Another reason the corporate-funded Right has targeted union members is that the more people there are in unions, the more progressive voters there are. In 2004, George W. Bush won white male voters by 25%—but lost by 21% among white males who belong to unions (a 46% swing). Bush won gun owners by 27%—but lost union-member gun owners by 12%. Regular church- goers went for Bush by a 22% margin, but union churchgoers went against Bush by 12%.

...need to explain why I say things." —President George W. Bush

SCARY STORY

John Graham is the kind of American hero we should all be proud of. He's served his country as a soldier, a diplomat, and now as a community-builder. He works tirelessly on The Giraffe Project (www.giraffe.org), helping kids stand up for themselves and their communities. So when we recieved this letter from him, we were shocked. It is, literally, incomprehensible to us that this could be happening in America. Here's what he wrote.

Heading for Oakland from Seattle to see my grandkids, the Alaska Airlines check-in machine refused to give me a boarding pass. Directed to the ticket counter, I gave the agent my driver's license and watched her punch keys at her computer.

Frowning, she told me that my name was on the national terrorist No-Fly Watch List and that I had to be specially cleared to board a plane. Any plane. Then she disappeared with my license for 10 minutes, returning with a boarding pass and a written notice from the Transportation Security Administration (TSA) confirming that my name was on a list of persons "who posed, or were suspected of posing, a threat to civil aviation or national security."

No one could tell me more than that. The computer was certain.

Back home in Seattle, I called the TSA's 800 number, where I rode a merry-go-round of pleasant recorded voices until I gave up. Turning to the TSA Web site, I downloaded a Passenger Identity Verification form that would assist the TSA in "assessing" my situation if I sent it in with a package of certified documents attesting to who I was.

I collected all this stuff and sent it in. Another 20 minutes on the phone to the TSA uncovered no live human being at all, let alone one who would tell me what I'd presumably done to get on The List. Searching my mind for possible reasons, I've been more and more puzzled. I used to work on national security issues for the

Ted Kennedy has been kept from boarding a plane 5 times. Reason: Potential terrorist.

State Department and I know how dangerous our country's opponents can be. To the dismay of many of my more progressive friends, I've given the feds the benefit of the doubt on homeland security. I tend to dismiss conspiracy theories as nonsense and I take my shoes off for the airport screeners with a smile.

I'm embarrassed that it took my own ox being gored for me to see the threat posed by the Administration's current restricting of civil liberties. I'm being accused of a serious—even treasonous—criminal intent by a faceless bureaucracy, with no opportunity (that I can find) to refute any errors or false charges. My ability to earn a living is threatened; I speak on civic action and leadership all over the world, including recently at the US Air Force Academy. Plane travel is key to my livelihood.

According to a recent MSNBC piece, thousands of Americans are having similar experiences. And this is not Chile under Pinochet. It's America. My country and yours.

With no real information to go on, I'm left to guess why this is happening to me. The easiest and most comforting guess is that it's all a mistake (a possibility the TSA form, to its credit, allows). But how? I'm a 63-year-old guy with an Anglo-Saxon name. I once held a Top Secret Umbra clearance (don't ask what it is but it meant the FBI vetted me up the whazoo for months). And since I left the government in 1980, my life has been an open book. It shouldn't be hard for the government to figure out that I'm not a menace to my country.

If they do think that, I can't see how. Since 1983, I've helped lead the Giraffe Heroes Project, a nonprofit that moves people to stick their necks out for the common good. In the tradition of Gandhi, King and Mandela, that can include challenging public policies people think are unjust. In 1990, the Project's founder and I were honored as "Points of Light" by the first President Bush for our work in fostering the health of this democracy. I've just written a book about activating citizens to get to work on whatever problems they care about, instead of sitting around complaining.

In 2004, singer Cat Stevens, now a Muslim named Yusuf Islam...

I'm also engaged in international peacemaking, working with an organization with a distinguished 60-year record of success in places ranging from post-war Europe to Africa. Peacemakers must talk to all sides, so over the years I've met with Cambodians, Sudanese, Palestinians, Israelis and many others. You can't convince people to move toward peaceful solutions unless you understand who they are.

As I said, I'm not into conspiracy theories. But I can't ignore this administration's efforts to purge and punish dissenters and opponents. Look, for example, at current efforts to cleanse PBS and NPR of "anti-administration" news. But I'm not Bill Moyers and the Giraffe Heroes Project is not PBS. We're a small operation working quietly to promote real citizenship.

Whether it's a mistake or somebody with the power to hassle me really thinks I am a threat, the stark absence of due process is unsettling. The worst of it is that being put on a list of America's enemies seems to be permanent. The TSA form states:

> "The TSA clearance process will not remove a name from the Watch Lists. Instead this process distinguishes passengers from persons who are in fact on the Watch Lists by placing their names and identifying information in a cleared portion of the Lists.

...which may or may not, the form continues, reduce the airport hassles." Huh?

My name is on a list of real and suspected enemies of the state and I can't find out what I'm accused of or why, let alone defend myself. And I'm guilty, says my government, not just until proven innocent or a victim of mistaken identity—but forever.

Sure, 9/11 changed a lot. Tougher internal security measures (like thorough screenings at airports and boundary crossings) are a dismal necessity. But, in protecting ourselves, we can't allow our leaders to continue to create a climate of fear and mistrust, to destroy our civil liberties and, in so doing, to change who we are as a nation. What a victory that would be for our enemies, and what a betrayal of real patriots and so many in the wider world

...was removed from a plane as soon as it arrived in the U.S.—and was immediately deported.

who still remember this country as a source of inspiration and hope.

I don't think it's like Germany in 1936—but, look at Germany in 1930. Primed by National Socialist propaganda to stay fearful and angry, Germans in droves refused to see the right's extreme views and actions as a threat to their liberties.

And don't forget that frog. You know that frog. Dropped into a pot of boiling water, he jumps out to safety. But put him into a pot of cold water over a steady flame, he won't realize the danger until it's too late to jump.

So how hot does the water have to get? When the feds can rifle through your library reading list? When they can intimidate journalists? When a government agency can keep you off airplanes without giving you a reason? When there's not even a pretense of due process? We're not talking about prisoners at Guantanamo; this is you and me. Well, after last week, it sure as hell is me and it could be you, next.

Oh, yes—Washington State just refused to renew my driver's license online, a privilege given others. I had to wait in line at the DMV before a computer decided I could drive home. This conspiracy theory debunker smells a connection to the Watch List.

I'm mobilizing everything I've got to challenge the government on this issue, in a country that I love and have served. Whatever your politics, it's your fight too. Yes, there needs to be a list of the bad guys, coordinated among the security agencies with a need-to-know. But we must demand that the government make public its criteria for putting people on this list—and those reasons can't include constitutionally protected dissent from government policies.

The feds can't be allowed to throw names on the list without first doing simple checks for mistaken identity. And no one's name should be added to the list, or kept on it, without a formal, open explanation of charges and the opportunity to challenge and disprove them. This assault on civil liberties must not stand—not for me, not for anybody.

"Scary Story" by John Graham ©1991–2005 Giraffe Heroes Project

RECOMMENDED READING

Here are some of the books we used for research. If we left out one of your favorites, please add it to the Reading List on our Web site (www.50simplethings.com).

Jerome Armstrong & Markos Moulitsas Zuniga, *Crashing the Gate: Netroots, Grassroots, and the Rise of People-Powered Politics*

Rob Boston, *Why the Religious Right Is Wrong: About Separation of Church & State,* and *Close Encounters With the Religious Right*

David Brock, *The Republican Noise Machine*

Adrienne Maree Brown & William Upski Wimsatt, ed., *How to Get Stupid White Men Out of Office*

Graydon Carter, *What We've Lost*

James Carville, *Had Enough?*

Forrest Church, Ed., *The Separation of Church and State: Writings On a Fundamental Freedom by America's Founders*

Willis Clint, *The I Hate Ann Coulter, Bill O'Reilly, Rush Limbaugh, Michael Savage, Sean Hannity... Reader*

Joe Conason, *Big Lies: The Right-Wing Propaganda Machine and How It Distorts the Truth*

Ellen Frank, *The Raw Deal: How Myths and Misinformation about the Deficit, Inflation, and Wealth Impoverish America*

Thomas Frank, *What's The Matter with Kansas*

Al Franken, *Lies and the Lying Liars Who Tell Them* and *The Truth with Jokes*

Ken Goodman, et al , *Saving Our Schools: The Case for Public Education*

Jacob S. Hacker, *Off Center: The Republican Revolution and the Erosion of American Democracy*

Don Hazen & Lakshmi Chaudry, ed., *Start Making Sense*

David Cay Johnston, *Perfectly Legal*

Dennis Loy Johnson & Valerie Merians, ed. *What We Do Now*

"If you always do what you always did...

Esther Kaplan, *With God on Their Side*

Robert F. Kennedy Jr., *Crimes Against Nature*

Isaac Kramnick & R. Laurence Moore, *The Godless Constitution: A Moral Defense of The Secular State*

George Lakoff, *Moral Politics: How Liberals and Conservatives Think, and Don't Think Of An Elephant*

Jan G. Linn, *What's Wrong with the Christian Right*

Mark Crispin Miller, *Fooled Again: How the Right Stole the 2004 Election*, and *Cruel and Unusual: Bush/Cheney's New World Order*

Anita Miller, *What Went Wrong In Ohio: The Conyers Report On The 2004 Presidential Election*

Bruce Miller, *Take Them at Their Words*

Chris Mooney, *The Republican War on Science*

Bill Press, *How the Republicans Stole Christmas*

Robert D. Putnam, *Bowling Alone: The Collapse And Revival Of American Community*

Sheldon Rampton & John Stauber, *Banana Republicans*, and *Toxic Sludge Is Good for You*

Robert Reich, *Reason: Why Liberals Will Win The Battle For America*

James Risen, *State of War: The Secret History of the C.I.A. and the Bush Administration*

Ed Schulz, *Straight Talk from the Heartland*

Felice Schwartz & Suzanne Levine, *The Armchair Activist*

Catherine Shaw, *The Campaign Manager: Running and Winning Local Elections*

David K. Shipler, *The Working Poor: Invisible In America*

Tavis Smiley, *Hard Left*

Joseph E. Stiglitz, *Globalization and Its Discontents*

Jim Wallis, *God's Politics: Why The Right Gets It Wrong And The Left Doesn't Get It*

Richard J. Weisman, *Fascists in Christian Clothing: The Vast Right Wing Conspiracy*

"...you'll always get what you always got."—Moms Mabley

THANK YOU

Earthworks Press sincerely thanks the community of people whose advice and assistance made this book possible. We've done our best to make sure everyone has been acknowledged but...just before this book went to press, our e-mail program crashed and many names were lost. We know that sounds a little like "The dog ate my homework," but it's true. So if we've left your name off this list...Our apologies. Please, let us know, so we can include your name in the next edition.

Sharon Javna	Jill Rothman	Peggy Wisneski
Jesse Javna	Jeremy Leaming	Bernie Horn
Sophie Javna	Michael Brunsfeld	Benjamin Zweig
Gordon Javna	Lorraine Bodger	Catalina Ruiz Healy
Claire and Steve	Alan Reder	Kirstin Falk
Brad Knickerbocker	James Adams	Deborah Schneider
Steve Baerman	Larry Cooper	Andrew Hoppin
Thom Little	Lenna Lebovitch	Kety Esquivel
Jeff Altemus	Ken Wells	Iara Peng
Susan Fassberg	Elyse Tischkoff	Laurie Boeder
Judy Plapinger	Kevin Davidson	Peter Murray
Claudia Bauer	John Stauber	Yolanda
Alexis Soulios	Doug Preston	Hippensteele
Jennifer Hart	Wade Dokken	Craig Aaron
Brian Boone	George Lakoff	Don Hazen
John Dollison	Carol Keys	Melissa Markell
John Graham	Mary Jean Collins	Jorge Mursuli
Nenelle Bunnin	Joel Barkin	Sergio Bendixen
Sue Carney	Simon Rosenberg	Ralph Miller
Chris Rose-Merkle	Joe Atkin	Celia Wexler
Steve Scholl	Peter Montgomery	Benjamin Rahn
Bill Tuck	Jim Fournier	Matt deBergalis
Scott Dalgarno	Andre Carothers	Hollie Ainbinder
Brad Bunnin	Mark Crispin Miller	Mark Ritchie
Douglas Ottati	Dan Carol	Rob Keithen
Shelley Epstein	Adrienne Maree	Bob Chase
Rob Boston	Brown	Erik Stowers
Raven Brooks	Jack Mingo	Matt Witt
Pamela Smith	Gloria Totten	Martha Ture

"In a time of universal deceit, telling the truth is a revolutionary act." —George Orwell

Chris Desser
Jeremy Funk
Page Gardner
Jim Gilliam
Molly Neitzel
Jim Gollin
Kari Chisholm
David Halperin
John Halpin
Holmes Wilson
Josh Wilson
Robert Greenwald
Markos Zuniga
Heather Merrill
Traci Siegel
Myles Weissleder
Ben Helphand
Peter Leyden
George Polisner
Theo Yedinsky
Gautam Raghavan
Brad de Graf
Eric Antebi
Kathy Spillar
Rebecca Moore
Dave Hawkins
Matthe McEnzie
Bill Moyer
Brent Bolton
Rick Mitchell
Al Robins
    & Jan Harrell
Kevin Wolf
Dean Roberts
Carly Miller
J. Potts
Loretta &
    Phil Schumacher
Ken Becker

Marcy Winograd
Ron Ferguson
Richard Seidman
Dan Suyeyasu
Ron Bagel
Leslie Liao
Susie Gilligan
Kim Spencer
Maria Cardona
Margie O'Driscoll
Jennifer Spoerri
Peter Teague
Van Jones
Justin Krebs
Ana Lefer
David Mathison
Jim Garrison
Rea Estelle
Julie Bergman Sender
Nancy Cunningham
Andrew Gillum
Jefferson Smith
Cathy Shaw
Becky Bond
Mary Beth Cahill
Casey Hill
Zack Rosen
Nicole Lazzaro
Katrina Wood
Emily Schwarz Greco
Marcia Conner
Susan Adelman
Jeff Chester
Jeff Cohen
Pam Costain
Terrence McNally
Bill Lofy
David Dill

Adam Werbach
Stephanie Schriock
Chris Canning
Marsha Zeesman
Dan Droller
Adam Borelli
Neal Gorenflo
Paul West
Medea Benjamin
Josh On
Jeff Blum
John Steiner
Jason Rosenberg
Eugenie Scott
Diane Mintz
Donna &
    Lee Chiacos
Ronit Roth
Diana Hartel
Paul Stanley
Janet Taggart
Adam Ruben
Annette Dow
Karen Sauer
Ann Vogel
Marianne Mollmann
Jean Doran
Cathy Holt
Kereth Lucker
Gertrude Fodiman
Peter Lee
Lana McGraw Boldt
Becca Neuwirth
Peter Wetherbee
Jane Slater
Ellen Dinerman
Michelle Hutchins
Pat Jobe
Jon Sarche

In 1970, Karl Rove tried to discredit a candidate by printing fliers on the man's letterhead reading...

Marla Estes
Joe Dully
Maureen Cannon
Keith Quick
Edward M. Aycock
Marilyn Zimmerman
Pattie Raynor
JM Causey
Karen Bouris
Kathleen Nichols
Molly Kurland
Lea Jones
Alan D. Moore
Stephanie Arrigotti
Geno Rodriguez
Erik Gronborg
Mary Zinn
Charlotte Horning
Lori Goldman
Joseph Richey
Cretia Shire
Bart Norman
David Berger
April McCaffery
Tom Hay
Cindy Garrison
Beth Hahn
Stephanie Hughes
Bill & Louise Brown
David Lewit
Carol Pettit
Elizabeth Gross
Beth Hahn
Liz Loescher
Peter &
   Trudy Johnson-Lenz
Mark Dubois
Gil Friend
Vivien Feyer

Rick Ingrasci M.D.
Paul Rerucha
Bob Stanley
Shelley Jarvis
Laura Hogan
Rebecca Muncy
Herman Heyn
Karen Cross
Paul Warner
Kathy Cuneo
Trudy Joyce
Marty Kurzfeld
Elaine P. Millen
Stephanie Sabar
Jean Doran
Mark Burch
Carol E. Roper
Michael Kinsley
Albert Kaufman
Larry Dobson
Susan Danzig
Susan Estrella
Christi Thomas
Malcolm Ferrier
Debbie Feldman-
   Jones
Nancy Newman
Marc Lionetti
Mark Sherman
Mimi Kennedy
M. Kila
Joy Marshall
Bobbie Burdett
Mia Van Meter
Mo Moss
Robert Mullen
Lowell Gilbertson
Sharon Goodwyn
Melanie Kelley

Ronald Harper
Patrick O'Heffernan
Nancy Davies
Jennifer Cannon
Nicolas A. Boillot
Kathleen Bridgewater
Katie Farrar
Charlotte Hubbell
Anesa Miller
Pim and Judy Ford-
   Brouwer
Suzanne Duarte
Parker Blackman
Zachary D. Weiser
Jill Wohrle
Tomye Kelley
Dorothy Bryant
Susan Albert Athas
Betty Schneider
Julie Bennett
Sherryanne Snipes
Richard Speer
Cindy Darnell
John Statler
Chris & Jim Abrams
Ed & Joann
   Houghton
Joel Dee
Kevin Mieras
Ed Greevy
Doug Fiske
John Koivula
Tor Bejnar
Peter Hansell
John D. Pearce
Valda Whitman
Merryl Weber
Gail James
Margaia Forcier-Call

...'free beer, free food, girls, and a good time for nothing.'"

Alaina Smith
Randy Schutt
Somer Waters
TP Flynn
John A. Cooper
Stephen Morris
Joe Kilikevice
R. Kohles
Bill Greenberg
Judy Brown
Berma Matteson
Nancy Duns
Philip Hough
Mark Cochran
David Goodwin
Herb &
   Merla Barberie
Ted Cheeseman
Kally Thurman
Kathryn Flynn
Darlene Pratt
Michelle Andrews
Marcia Eaton
Marianne Scruggs
Kathy Loehmer
Susan Saxton
   D'Aoust
Lois Murphy
William Albright
James J. Godsil
Margaret Keng
Margaret Schultz
Ann Medlock
Tim Buckley
Evalyn Bemis
William Albright
Mike Henderson
Thomas Boyd

William Sell
Stuart Gunter
Elizabeth Hancock
Chuck Sheketoff
Daniel Goodman
Kelly Jacobs
Kristina Goldberg
Chris Vose
Lauri Berkenkamp
Sally Seymour
Lisa Rosenthal
Janet Monville
Colin Stuart
Judi Demucci
Gerilee Hundt
L.J. Balance
J. Well
Ann Reavey
William Landers
David Drake
Anna Lee Alvarez
Susan McMullin
Harvey Kaltsas
Bob Wilson
M. Qutierrezec
Sandie Goodwin
Shelley Schou
Katey Branch
Martha Weinstein
Greg Palast
Rita Weinstein
Stephen Morris
Marta Green & Rod
Frank Watanabe
Ken Jopp
Jerome Rosen
Jackie Marcus
Shelley and Koby

Dunlap
Dr. Vicki Watson
Max Harper
Donna L. Jones
John Longenbaugh
Wendy Kurland
Stephen Morri
Suzanne McQueen
Deborah Steelwright
Cecil Bothwell
Kathy Shayler
Shannon Lee
Usta Run
Lloyd Chapman &
   Susan
Tracy L'Herisson
Shelly M. Mcfarland
Susan Powning
Harry L. Cass
Dorothy Field
Jason Elmendorf
Rebecca Banyas
Randy Paynter
Vicky Husband
Thierry Chouard
Jo Salas
Sharon Hudgins
Stuart Sherman
Kathleen Rosenblatt
Christine Perala
   Gardiner
Bill Kauth
Ruth Mason
Elizabeth Brady
Roy Ceres
Sheryl Sackman
Robin Diener
Robert Ferrew

Republican messaging: "Never say 'Tax Reform.' Always say 'Tax Simplification.'"

Jeanne Callahan
Courtney L Dillard
Marie Kelleher-Roy
Scott Walsh
Amanda Smith
Carsten Henningsen
Sandy Mitchell
Joann Navickas
W. Fudeman
Nina Ahry
Jane Marie Law
John Himmelfarb
Wendy Brawer
Steve & Mia Harper
Robin Herskowitz
Mary Ellen Aguirre
Lynn Landry
Paul Copeland
Bruce Morehouse
Andrea Lalime
Bob Mayer
Sherry Bohlen
Rob Stein
Eileen Bayers
Jeff Berman
Alicia Viani
Will Wilkinson

Bruce Borgerson
Ron Ferguson
Deborah Steele
Nancy Bloom
John & Melissa
    Mitchell-Hooge
Nina Salomon
Sunny Spicer
Kim Nathanson
Deborah Mokma
Shari Steele
Paul Lipke
Lola Wilcox
Jeff Cheek
John Fricker
Heather Booth
Brent Bolton
George Greenwald
Lura Astor
Evan Sugden
Jon Lange
Angela Garcia
Combs
Lisa Karst
David Chandler
Arlo Leach
Ryan Langemeyer

Scott Branchfield
Joy Marshall
Elizabeth Garzarelli
Melanie Kelley
Megan Matson
Diane Ferchel
Kevin Wolf
Susan Strong
Brian Lewis
Laura Flanders
Cindy Mazzei
Tom Collina
Joe Conason
Steven Marshank
Barry Turkus
Catherine Dee
George Mastoras
Ted Gambordella
Gary Pool
Vince Mazzi
Bev Harris
Don Parker
Jane Hamsher
Dan Schmitz
Kristine Hemp
Lynn Christel
David Neiwert

Home of the Luntzie Awards: www.Luntzspeak.com

Watch Keith Olbermann on MSNBC

Read *The Onion*: www.theonion.com

Watch Jon Stewart and Stephen Colbert on Comedy Central

Watch Link TV: *www.worldlinktv.org*

Investigative reporting: *www.exxonsecrets.org*

50simplethings.com

Well, the book's done, but we feel as though we've just gotten started. Things are happening so fast in the progressive community, and so much information is becoming available, that there's no way we're ever going to get it all down on paper.

So…we're making the 50 Simple Things Web site our next project. By the time you read this, it will (hopefully) be up and running. We want *50simplethings.com* to be a liberal activist's site—one you and other progressives can go to when you want to share, learn, or just talk about the things you're doing in your daily life to build a better America.

We hope you'll visit us and …

• **Tell your story.** Which of the 50 Simple Things have you tried? What happened?

• **Chat with other people** who are trying to make a difference about what works and what doesn't.

• **Be an inspiration.** There are thousands of progressive Americans doing impressive things for their country. By sharing what you know, you'll be helping to build the progressive movement.

• **Share new links.** There's amazing information available about each of the 50 Things. As we discover new links and articles, we'll add them to the site.

• **Help us with updates and corrections.** Have things changed? Did we get something wrong? With your help, we'll update the book with every new printing. And between printings, readers will be able to find any changes by checking the site.

…And a lot more. We'll probably be just as surprised by what we come up with as you will. In any case, we hope to see you there at *50simplethings.com*